THE COLD CALLING EQUATION

PROBLEM SOLVED

MICHAEL HALPER

ISBN: 1468173545
ISBN 13: 9781468173543

Library of Congress Control Number: 2012900265
CreateSpace, North Charleston, SC

"The Cold Calling Equation is both easy to understand and thorough. While Michael lays out winning tactics specific to cold calling, he's also framed these techniques within the fundamental principles of consultative selling. Those who adopt the concepts in this book are ensured of increased success in sales and improved peace of mind."

CRAIG KLEIN
– CEO, SALESNEXUS.COM

"I highly recommend this book to anyone looking for a practical and effective approach to prospecting. Michael covers all of the important tactics and strategies to achieve great cold calling results."

JEREMY ULMER
– PRESIDENT, SALESCOACHINGHABITS.COM

"If you want to transform your prospecting activity into high-performing executable results, you picked the right book. The Cold Calling Equation does a great job of articulating a core methodology, but most importantly provides an easy-to-use playbook and guide to take action immediately. The concepts and ideas in this book are sound approaches for sales professionals at any skill level."

MIKE KINNEY
– EXECUTIVE VP OF SALES, ASURE SOFTWARE

"Most books about cold calling just focus on tactics. In The Cold Calling Equation, Michael Halper digs further to address not only tactics, but also strategies, planning, and, perhaps most importantly, the mental state of the sales person. Most people will never enjoy cold calling, but that doesn't mean they can't be successful at it. Michael addresses the challenges of cold calling directly and shows how to make it a successful component of a sales strategy."

RUSTY SMITH
– PRESIDENT, THE CENTER FOR GROWTH

"The great thing about this book is that it can help anybody to improve results regardless of sales experience. This book would be great for the technical-minded sales person and entrepreneur."

COREY PRATOR
– CEO, RENT YOUR CIO

"A comprehensive yet concise framework that can help any sales person to immediately improve results. This book could be used to develop a corporate cold calling program or improve an existing one."

ANDREA NICHOLAS
- CEO, OPTIMIZE PROJECT MANAGEMENT

TABLE OF CONTENTS

1

INTRODUCTION

TAKING THE FIRST
STEP FORWARD

*A journey of a thousand miles
begins with a single step.*

Lao-tzu

The great thing about sales, and more specifically cold calling, is that it truly is a skill. It is a skill because there are clear things that we can learn and do, or not do, to impact our results and effectiveness. We can consciously adopt different techniques, philosophies, and methodologies and likely see an immediate impact on our results. This is good news, as it means that we have a great amount of control over our results and our success. If we want to get better results, in most cases we can invest time and energy in learning and developing this skill and likely see a return on our investment in the form of improved sales performance and increased sales.

HARD WORK ≠ SALES RESULTS

There are many jobs where hard work and extra effort will typically lead to some amount of results. Digging a ditch, for example. If we were digging a ditch, regardless of how we positioned our hands on the shovel, or the type of motion and form that we used during the digging stroke, if we worked really hard for a period of time, we would likely see some amount of progress and productivity. Even if there is a more efficient method, the hard work will compensate for poor form and get us some amount of progress toward our goal.

Unfortunately, or maybe fortunately depending on your point of view, this is not the case when working as a sales professional. In the world of sales, working hard alone does not always translate into success. This is not to discount the importance of hard work, as there can definitely be a correlation between top performers and hard work. But we can make 100 cold calls every day, and if we use the wrong form and technique, we could actually see zero results from all of that hard work. Sales is tough, and there are simply no points given out for trying really hard while not using the right techniques and processes.

To demonstrate this premise, if we are successful with filling our calendar with meetings with prospects, we would feel and look very busy and productive. But if the prospects whom we are meeting with are not qualified in terms of having a true need to purchase, having the authority to make a purchase, or having the ability to make a purchase from a funding standpoint, we could be working hard with prospects who do not have a real probability of purchasing. This means that all of our hard work and busyness might produce very little actual sales and, in this instance, all of our hard work will not be leading to an equal amount of sales results.

The good news in all of this is that if we use the right techniques and tactics, we can improve both our effectiveness and efficiency. This means that if we develop our knowledge and skills, not only can we stand to improve the amount of results that we get from the work that we put in, but when we get really sharp, we stand to find ourselves in scenarios where we exceed expectations with average levels of effort.

HOW THIS BOOK CAN HELP

This book is designed to help improve the form and technique that a sales person will use when making cold calls. The concepts in this book are very easy and practical to implement, making them adoptable by any sales person regardless of skill level and experience. The suggested changes in this book can lead to an immediate improvement in cold calling results, which can lead to both better quality and better quantity leads in the short-term. In the long-term, the impact from these improvements can be an increase in overall sales and improved sales performance.

RETIRE A TRADITIONAL FORMULA

Before we move to outline what this book will focus on, let's first look at one of the most common formulas for improving sales performance or cold calling results: the sales funnel concept.

The sales funnel is a formula that is built on the premise that you put in some amount of lead generation activity into the top of the funnel, like hours of cold calling for example, and out of that investment you will have a certain number of conversations. Out of those conversations, you will schedule a certain number of appointments. Out of the appointments that you execute, you will produce a certain number of leads. A certain percentage of those leads should close in the form of sales, and this is what comes out of the bottom of the funnel.

That is the sales funnel. The math and logic are all sound, but there are three pitfalls that we can easily encounter when we are only focused on the funnel:

1. Assuming effort = results

If we fully subscribe to the sales funnel concept, then we have the expectation that putting in some sort of activity into the top of the funnel will lead to some amount of results. The challenge with that expectation is that, as we already pointed out, effort alone is not guaranteed to lead to any results. If our technique, form, or messaging is off and we put an investment of lead generation activity into the top of the funnel, our expectation of results might not be met as very little or nothing could come out of the bottom of the sales funnel. As a result, the sales funnel concept by itself could be a poor model to use to improve results and establish sales expectations.

2. Assuming ratios should be the same for everybody

Another pitfall that we can fall into is believing that the conversion ratios throughout the sales funnel are somewhat fixed and should be the same for everybody. Essentially, there could be the belief that everyone on the sales team should have the same conversion rates in terms of creating conversations from cold calls, converting conversations to meetings, and converting leads to closed deals.

There are many factors involved in every sale, and every sales person is unique in terms of style and ability. So it would be fairly unrealistic to expect different members of a sales team to have the same conversion rates throughout the different segments of the sales funnel. There may be some team members that are great at getting appointments yet have a lower close rate. And others that create less appointments but close more of the prospects that they meet with. These two different types of sales reps could end up with the same amount of closed business yet have very different shaped sales funnels. As a result, a static set of funnel ratios might not be the most effective model to use to develop and manage a team of diverse and dynamic sales resources.

3. Only looking at the top of the funnel

In addition, we can also get hung up on assuming that the conversion rates are what they are and that there is not a whole lot that we can do to improve them individually. In other words, it can be common to believe that hit rates, lead rates, and close rates are somewhat fixed and that the main variable that we need to focus on and manage is the activity level that is put into the top of the funnel. We need more sales, so we throw more callers and more actual dials at the problem.

While the top of the sales funnel is important and we definitely need to make calls, only focusing on the effort that is put in can be flawed on the basis that if our message or our technique is off, we could just be doing more of a misdirected approach, and the extra effort might not yield results and could be a waste of time and money. If we only focus on trying to achieve more by simply doing more, we could be missing a tremendous amount of opportunity.

A NEW FORMULA

This book introduces a new formula that focuses on looking more at the inside of the sales funnel and focuses on all of the individual steps and mechanics of cold calling to improve effectiveness and sales results. The formula looks at activity as well, but that is not the main variable that is focused on. The strategy is to improve sales results by getting the most out of the activity that we are making, as opposed to trying to improve sales results by only increasing activity.

This formula breaks down the steps or mechanics of cold calling into different variables. Those variables are then broken down individually to identify what to do and what not to do with each. We then put those variables together to create the *Cold Calling Equation*. With this model, we can then learn about and improve each variable individually and as a result, we can solve the equation and solve the common problem of how to consistently achieve results cold calling.

VARIABLES OF THE COLD CALLING EQUATION

We will go through each variable one at a time, but below is a list of the variables of the Cold Calling Equation:

+ Goal
+ Value
+ Target
+ Qualify
+ Objections
+ Disqualify
+ Gatekeeper
+ Pain
+ Interest

+ Rapport
+ Credibility
+ Script
+ Inner Game
+ Activity
+ Voice
+ Connect
+ Email
+ Voicemail
+ Closing
+ Reflection
= Sum

SECTION I

STRATEGY

2

GOAL

FOCUSING ON THE BEST GOAL

Begin with the end in mind.

STEPHEN COVEY

As you begin to try to improve your cold calling, a good place to begin is to stop and focus on what your primary goal of each call is. To improve results and consistency, it can be very helpful to have a very clear idea of what exactly you are trying to achieve. You need to have a clear picture of where you are trying to go in order to improve your chances of getting there.

This topic is worth discussing, as it is easy to get lured into chasing larger goals that are sometimes too ambitious for a cold call. For example, a sales person may try to fully sell the prospect on his products or services during the cold call. But since a cold call should only last between two to five minutes, this might not be the best time to try to achieve so much. If you identify what the best goal for the time and space that you have to work with is and focus solely on that, you can stand to improve your results.

DEFINITION OF A COLD CALL

Before we move forward, let's clearly define exactly what a cold call is, as it could differ from sales person to sales person. For the purposes of this book, a cold call is a call that you make in which the person you are calling is not expecting your call and does not know who you are. That being the case, most of these conversations should last, as just mentioned, between two to five minutes. If the cold call goes beyond that, you are either moving too slowly and are going to start to lose the prospect's attention or you have progressed beyond the cold call and moved on to the first conversation stage of the sales cycle.

Another label or way to look at a cold call is that it is the first contact that you have with the prospect. With using the label of first contact, you could also apply a lot of the tactics and principles in this book when receiving inbound calls from prospects. While calls where the prospect calls you are much easier than outbound cold calls, you can still stand to improve your effectiveness by treating those as a cold call or first contact and use some of the principles that will be discussed later in this book like qualifying, finding pain, building interest, and more.

DEFINITION OF A FIRST CONVERSATION

We use a concept of "first conversation" in this book to refer to the stage of the sales cycle that is just beyond the cold call. This is a point at which both the prospect and sales person have expressed interest and agreement in talking more. This differs from a cold call in that during a cold call, only the sales person will have interest in talking. Once the sales person gets the prospect's attention and there is a verbal or implied agreement to continue, the sales process has just transitioned from the cold call to the first conversation.

The first conversation can happen at the same time as the cold call (technically, right after) but a more effective approach can be to confirm agreement in talking and transition toward getting back together at a scheduled time on another day and setting an appointment to meet with the prospect. This type of transition can allow both the prospect and the sales person to regroup and better prepare for the conversation.

A first conversation could take on many different shapes as it could be a simple conversation over the phone, a casual conversation in person, or it could have more structure and be a presentation, demonstration, or scheduled event. Other labels that could be used for the first conversation are first call, first meeting, first appointment, etc.

It is important to know the difference between a cold call and first conversation and where the line is drawn between the two, as there are different tactics, processes, and goals that can be applied to each.

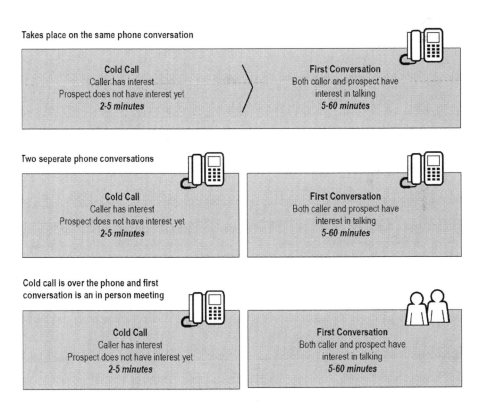

Takes place on the same phone conversation

Cold Call
Caller has interest
Prospect does not have interest yet
2-5 minutes

First Conversation
Both caller and prospect have interest in talking
5-60 minutes

Two seperate phone conversations

Cold Call
Caller has interest
Prospect does not have interest yet
2-5 minutes

First Conversation
Both caller and prospect have interest in talking
5-60 minutes

Cold call is over the phone and first conversation is an in person meeting

Cold Call
Caller has interest
Prospect does not have interest yet
2-5 minutes

First Conversation
Both caller and prospect have interest in talking
5-60 minutes

THE BEST GOAL OF A COLD CALL

Since a cold call may only last between two to five minutes, you need to identify the best goal to focus on. While the best goal for your first conversation can vary according to the business that you are in and product that you sell, in many cases the best goal of a cold call is to get the prospect transitioned to the first conversation. In other words, the best goal of the cold call is to schedule a meeting or appointment with the prospect to talk in more detail.

At the simplest level, if you can shift your mindset from trying to fully sell the prospect on your products or services during the cold call and focus on trying to get the prospect to have a conversation in which both parties are interested in talking, you can likely see a positive impact on your results.

One of the main reasons that this subject is worth pointing out is that it can be easy for us to always be in the selling or closing gear, especially when you factor in quotas and targets looming over our heads, and add to that the need to provide for ourselves and for our families. The "always be closing" mindset is great, except for the fact that a cold call does not provide enough time and attention from the prospect for us to be able to completely sell our products and services. If we don't consciously stop and internally recognize that we should not try to sell anything at this point, we can easily fall into the internal trap of trying to achieve too much during a cold call.

By establishing the internal focus of not trying to completely sell the prospect and shifting toward just trying to start a real conversation where both sides are interested and contributing, you can not only improve your focus and direction, but you can also greatly improve your appearance to your prospects. This will allow you to both verbally and nonverbally communicate the message of "I am not trying to sell anything to you at this point. I don't even know if what we have is a fit for you. I am simply looking to open the lines of communication between our two organizations and learn a little more about where you are today." That is not only a much more powerful message, it is also a much less threatening message, and one that is a lot harder for a prospect to object to. For example, when a prospect that tries to get rid of you by giving an objection that she is not interested, cannot change anything right now, or does not have any budget, she will have a much more difficult time ending the conversation if you carry yourself as not trying to sell anything.

When we add all of that up, confirming that the prospect is willing to keep talking and moving on to a first conversation is the best goal in many cold calling situations, and getting this agreement from prospects can be the first sale that we can focus on making. Once we progress to a first conversation, we will have more time and attention from the prospect and can then begin to talk in more detail and work toward larger and more ambitious goals.

HAVING A PLAN B

Regardless of how well you execute, you will not reach your primary goal on every cold call. With that being the case, it can be very advantageous to have a "plan B" or secondary goal when the call does not go in the preferred direction.

If the primary goal of the cold call is to secure a first conversation, below are some examples of good secondary goals to focus on when the prospect does not agree to move forward:

- Secure email address
- Get permission to add to newsletter
- Send email with additional information
- Collect current environment details
- Collect organizational details
- Collect contact info for other key players
- Get an internal referral

3

VALUE

GRAB THE PROSPECT'S ATTENTION

Price is what you pay. Value is what you get.

WARREN BUFFETT

In order to improve cold calling, not only is it critical for you to be able to grab the prospect's attention, but you have to do so in a very short space of time. One way to improve your effectiveness in this area is to improve your ability to clearly communicate the value that you have to offer.

WHAT IS VALUE?

Before we go any further, let's stop to try to define exactly what value is in the context that we use it as the meaning can vary in different situations.

When we talk about value, we are referring to the transfer of something from one party to another that has a positive net worth. Now, the important thing to get your hands around with this is that value is an intangible attribute. It is not something you can see or pick up, yet it is definitely there, and it always has a positive net worth.

Value is something that is transferred every day at a personal level between family and friends. For example, when you bring humor to a group or conversation and make someone laugh, you are providing value as you are improving the conversation. Other examples of providing value at a personal level may be teaching someone something, being a good listener, providing security, or making someone's life easier. In all of these examples, you are contributing something that is intangible with a positive net worth to another person.

Once you understand how you offer value at a personal level, you can better understand how you deliver value at a business level. Just as you can improve the lives and interactions with friends and family, you can also contribute value to your clients and you do this by making things work better, helping them to save or make money, and helping them to achieve more.

One important thing to start to get your hands around is that value is not the same thing as the product that you provide. Value is what your product helps your clients to do or what it helps them to achieve.

THREE LEVELS OF VALUE

The value that you deliver can typically impact your clients on three different levels – technical, business, and personal.

Technical Value

At the lowest level, you offer technical value. These are the benefits and improvements that you can deliver that make things work better and are realized in areas like of processes, systems, and people. Here are some examples of delivering value at the technical level:

- Helping a business to save time
- Automating certain manual tasks

- Improving the performance of system, processes, or people
- Improving the reliability of system, processes, or people

Business Value

As a business begins to realize value at the technical level, those benefits will work their way up and create value at the business level. This value can be seen in areas like of revenue, costs, and services. Here are some examples of businesses realizing value at the business level:

- Increases in revenue
- Market share growth
- Improvement in close rate
- Decrease in cost of goods sold
- Decrease in inventory cost
- Decrease in labor costs
- Improvement in customer satisfaction
- Decrease in product delivery time

Personal Value

The technical and business value that we deliver can continue to work its way up and impact clients at a personal level. Personal value can be seen in areas like income, career, and work environment. Here are some examples of prospects realizing value at the personal level:

- Increases in bonuses or commissions
- Improved probability for promotion
- Performance recognition
- Decrease in workload
- Decrease in stress level
- Improve work/life balance

WHY VALUE IS IMPORTANT

Now that you understand a little more about what exactly value is, let's discuss why it is so important.

Grab the Prospect's Attention

First, in any sales setting, it is critical to get the prospect's attention and by shifting from talking about your products to talking more about the value that you have to offer will help with this. One reason for this is that you will be communicating in a language that is closer to one that the prospect understands.

To elaborate on that a bit, when you talk about your products or services, you lean toward speaking in a language that you understand very well as you live and breathe this stuff. Not only have you likely gone through product training, but you are also exposed to this stuff every day. Yet this language or topic might be a little foreign to the prospect and as result, they may be a less engaged when that is all that you talk about. But when you focus on the technical, business, and personal benefits that you offer, you will shift to a language that the prospect is more familiar with and, as a result, there is a great chance for you to grab his attention and create a more engaging conversation.

In addition, when you focus more on value, you shift from talking about your company and your products, which is a very "all about me" conversation and you shift more toward talking about the prospect and his interests and needs. We are all a little self-serving and by keeping the conversation more on the prospect and less on you can help make the prospect more involved and attentative.

Another thing to keep in mind with trying to get and keep the prospect's attention is that when he answers a cold call, he is most likely not in shopping mode. This is a safe assumption because the prospect is likely not sitting there thinking about purchasing what you have to offer at the particular time that he answers your call. As result, when you focus solely on your products, you might not talk about something that he cares about at that particular moment. But if you focus on the value that you have to offer, you increase your odds of talking about something that he is interested in and, as a result, you are more likely to grab his attention.

Improve the Impression You Make

When you are able to focus more on value, you are likely to give off a much better impression to the prospect. This is because many of the other sales professionals will be primarily talking about their products and services and you will immediately stand out from the pack and seem more knowledgeable and polished as you are aware the value that you offer and the value that the prospect cares about.

Build Interest

We've talked about how communicating value will help to grab the prospect's attention. That is great but at some point you will need to take that from having his attention to having his interest and incorporating value into what you discuss will help you to be more effective at this. You can have the best technology available, but if you do not communicate what that means to the prospect in terms of value, you might not trigger any interest.

IDENTIFYING YOUR VALUE

The first step with improving your ability to communicate value is to clearly identify the value that you have to offer. Here is a step-by-step process that you can go through to map out your value:

Step 1: Identify a product or service that you offer

Identify a product or service that you sell. If you want to get more granular with this exercise or if you only sell one product, you could use one of the features of your product in this step.

Step 2: Identify what your product does

Try to write out a quick description about what your product does from a functional standpoint. One sentence that explains what takes place in very simple language is sufficient for this exercise.

Step 3: Identify how your product helps at a technical level

When a customer or client uses your product, how does this help them at the technical level? Remember that these are the improvements that you help to create in areas like processes, systems, and people. Think about how your product might help those areas and try to put together one sentence that describes that. This is the technical value that you offer.

Step 4: Identify how your product helps at a business level

The next step is to identify how the technical value that you identified will work its way up and impact the client from a business standpoint. When the technical improvements begin to take shape, how will that impact the business? Think about areas like revenue, costs, and services. Try to write one sentence that summarizes these business improvements. This is the business value that you offer.

Step 5: Identify how your product helps at a personal level

The technical and business value that you offer can lead to improvements at a personal level for your clients. Try to think about how these improvements will impact a client in the areas of income, career, and work environment and try to formulate a brief sentence that describes possible improvements. This is the personal value that you offer.

Step 6: (Optional) Repeat for other products

What you just outlined may give you enough value points to work with when trying to improve the way you communicate the value you have to offer. If you want to continue the exercise and be more thorough, you can go through steps 1 through 5 again for other products, services, or features that you sell.

Step 7: (Optional) Summarize to arrive at core value

If you add additional products, you are going to come up with a number of different statements that describe what you do and how you help. This is good information but will likely be too much to share when interacting with prospects during a cold call. One step that you can take to help with that is to group all of the technical, business, and personal points together and then try to summarize or group them together to get to single statements that quickly explain what the core technical, business, and personal value that you offer is. If there is not a real good way to summarize, you can pick one of the individual points that is either dominant or more attention grabbing. These summary points become the core value that you offer.

CREATE A VALUE STATEMENT

Now that you have identified descriptions that detail the value that you have to offer, you can take those and create a value statement. A value statement is a sentence that cleanly and concisely summarizes the value that transfers from you to your clients when they use your products or services.

An example of a short value statement is "We help companies to improve sales revenue from new clients and we do this by improving the areas of prospecting and cold calling." This statement is brief, clearly explains the value that we have to offer, and can be easily rattled off early in a cold call or conversation.

Common Pitfalls with Value Statements

Whether they realize it or not, many sales people automatically add in some sort of value statement to their pitch. However, sometimes what we think is a value statement can end up off-track by falling into some common pitfalls.

The Ole Company Description

One of the most common challenges with value statements that naturally roll off of the tongue is that they can often turn out to be more of a company introduction statement.

For example, "I am with XG Corp. We are a global company and we provide the most advanced office printers on the market." This is not a value statement. This is more of a company description statement stating where the company operates, what it sells, and how the sales person perceives that her products match up against the competition. This statement does not tell the prospect the benefits he stands to gain by doing business with the company that sales person represents.

A prospect who receives a cold call and is currently not looking to make a purchase will likely not care that the company calling them is a global company and that it may have the best product on the market.

Too Focused on Products and Features

Another pitfall that may occur with value statements is that we can often focus on talking about our products and features when we are trying to describe the value that we have to offer. For example, "I am with Secure Site and we provide ultra-sensitive motion detection equipment." This statement is informative, but it does not include any of the value that is offered.

Falling into this trap is very understandable. As sales people, we often know our products and features inside and out, and we can get easily excited about an opportunity to talk about them. But when we do not include or focus on the value that we offer, we may end up not grabbing the prospect's attention or talking about what he ultimately cares about.

Getting too Fancy

One last thing to be careful of is that it can be easy to get too fancy with the value statement by using large, sophisticated words. For example, "We are the industry leading provider of pipe connection solutions. Our cutting edge solutions help to unify ventricular flows to optimize strategic liquid placement and transportation." This value statement definitely communicates some of the value offered and this might be great language for a brochure or website. But the value statements that we are building here are typically delivered verbally in sales situations. When you use working like "industry leading" and "optimize strategic liquid placement", you begin to sound a little too rehearsed and that can decrease your level of authenticity.

Value Statement Templates

The following are templates that allow you to take the individual value points that you produced and easily just insert them into the template to produce a variety of value statements.

Short and Sweet

We help [Insert whom you help—business, individuals, law firms, hospitals, HR managers, etc.] to [insert technical, business or personal value].

Examples

"We help doctor's office to decrease the rate of patient no-shows."

"We help small businesses to improve their revenue from new clients."

"We help VP's of sales to improve their overall annual commissions."

Connect Technical Value with Business Value

We help [Insert whom you help] to [insert technical value] and this typically leads to [insert business value].

Examples

"We help businesses to manage their sales pipeline better and this typically leads to a higher close rate and sales revenue."

"We help IT departments to improve their visibility across their IT infrastructure and this can typically lead to better delivery of business services."

"We help businesses to improve their ability to effectively manage their inventory levels and this often leads to a decrease in cost of goods sold."

Connect Business Value with Technical Value

We help [Insert whom you help] to [insert business value] and do this by [insert technical value].

Examples

"We help businesses to grow their new logo clients and do this by improving their outbound sales activities."

"We help IT manufacturing companies to decrease labor costs and do this by helping them to improve their ability schedule resources."

"We help operations managers to improve their management of their P&L and do this by providing real-time materials reporting."

Connect the Product with Value

We provide [Insert your product] and this helps [Insert whom you help] to [insert technical, business, or personal value].

Examples

"We provide inventory management software and this helps businesses to control and decrease their cost of goods sold."

"We provide custom cabinets and this helps homeowners to design a kitchen that they are sure to be happy with."

"We provide IT outsourcing services and this helps businesses to improve the reliability of their internal IT services."

When to Use a Value Statement

Once a value statement is created, you can use it at many different times during the sales cycle. Whether you are cold calling prospects, delivering presentations, or putting together proposals, there are many different times where you can improve your effectiveness by being able to clearly and concisely communicate the value that you have to offer.

When trying to improve cold calling results, if you deliver your value statement at the beginning of the call when you introduce yourself, you can not only improve your ability to get the prospect's attention, but you will also be telling her why she should spend the next two to five minutes talking with you. The very first sale that you need to close is trying to sell the prospect on stopping what she is doing to take a brief call from you. And a good value statement will improve your results in closing that first mini-sale.

4

TARGET

DEFINING THE IDEAL PROSPECT

If eighty percent of your sales come from twenty percent of all of your items, just carry those twenty percent.

HENRY A. KISSINGER

Whether you are working as a sales professional or as a business owner, it is critical to effectively manage your time. One of the reasons this is so important is that time is a resource that cannot be replaced. While we can usually order more supplies, borrow more money, or hire more resources, we are not able to buy more time or add more hours to the day. That being the case, you must get the most out of the time that you have to work with. One way to help with this is to figure out which prospects you should spend your valuable time with.

IDEAL PROSPECT CHARACTERISTICS

In order to increase the time spent with good prospects and decrease time spent with not-so-great prospects, it can help to stop and identify what your ideal prospect looks like. While you can likely sell your products and services to just about everybody, or at least to a very large market, there is likely a segment that you fit best with. Try to identify this segment and the characteristics that comprise it so you can then build the profile for your ideal prospect.

Some of the key characteristics that you can consider when trying to identify what your ideal prospect looks like are industry, geography, company size, current state, and title.

Industry

When working to define the ideal prospect, you can look to see if there is an industry that your core value matches up best with. In some scenarios, this may be very clear. For example, if a product sold can only be used by a local government entity, then that clearly is the industry for the ideal prospect.

But in some cases, a product could be used by many or all industries. When this is the case, you can look to the industries in which the value realized by consuming your products or services is high or higher than others. If a prospect from one industry can benefit more than a prospect from another industry, you may want to target the prospect who has the most to gain because she might have a higher probability of not only closing for the initial purchase, but she will also have a higher probability of returning to buy again compared to other prospects where the value realized is less.

Another characteristic you may want to consider when examining industry is that prospects from one industry may have a higher ability to purchase or ease of doing business with compared to another. For example, we may be able to sell our products to government entities, but either due to red tape or economic conditions, it may be more time consuming and difficult to get a transaction executed in that industry compared to a prospect from the private sector. These may be secondary characteristics to look at to try to narrow down the industry or industries for your ideal prospect.

If it is difficult to narrow down the industry or industries that you should focus on, you can come at it from the other side and look at which industries it makes sense to exclude. For example, if our products do not fit well with hospitals, schools, and government agencies but fit well with pretty much all other industries, we can use those exclusion details to tighten the industry focus for our ideal prospect. In other words, instead of focusing on only selling to three particular industries, we will focus on selling to all but remove three industries that do not fit well as our approach to tighten up what our ideal prospect looks like.

Geography

The world is a big place and you cannot be everywhere, so it can help to narrow down the target geographic area for your cold calling and identify what areas will have the biggest concentrations of ideal prospects.

A lot of this work may already have been completed for you if you are part of a sales team, as your sales management might have assigned you with a territory to be responsible for. Even if this is the case, you can still sometimes stand to narrow down the total territory that you have to work with to identify which geographic areas of prospects you can benefit from most.

For example, your territory or area that you can do business in might be an entire state or set of states. Even though you have that entire area to work with, it might not make sense to canvas that entire area when cold calling. To optimize your time, you can identify where the biggest concentrations of ideal prospects exist and which areas it makes sense to include as part of your target area.

Company Size

You might want to do business with companies of all sizes and prefer to do business with the largest of organizations. However, your business and the products you sell might not fit well with companies of all sizes, and even if they did, it would not be a great strategy to go after all of them.

One thing to consider is that you may sell a product that does not scale up and work well with large businesses. Or you may sell a product that delivers tremendous value, but it does not make sense from a financial standpoint and is cost-prohibitive for small organizations. These types of factors will influence what size of company you should target.

Annual revenue and employee count are good metrics to use when determining the size of companies to focus on. For example, it may be determined that companies of between $100 million and $1 billion annual revenue is your sweet spot and the key characteristic for the size range for your ideal prospects. An example of using employee count would be to arrive at a range of 2,500 to 10,000 total employees for your ideal prospects.

Organizational Details

A key part of identifying the ideal prospect is to identify the best title or individual that you should connect with during your prospecting. First, identify what functional areas inside of the prospect's organization it makes the most sense to focus on. This will either be the department that will purchase your products and services, or it could also be a department that could be impacted by the use of your products. For example, we may sell a software solution that is used by finance. In this scenario, it could be the case that we want to call into both finance and IT as both functional areas will be impacted and involved in a purchase.

From there, determine what level of the organization that it makes the most sense to call. Are you going to call into lower or user levels of the organization, mid-level management, or are you going to try to connect at a senior management level? The answer should be a little of all three. The lower levels are not only usually more accessible, they also have valuable current state information. But we will need to include the appropriate levels of management in our calling as those are the individuals that will be more involved in the approval and decision making process.

Current State

One of the most important characteristics to identify is the ideal current state or current environment for your ideal prospect. In this context, current state refers to the details of the prospect's activities and setup in the area where the products and services that you sell fit. This could include details about current systems, existing processes, current contracts, current providers, etc.

For example, if your company sells a particular business service such as IT outsourcing, it could be more productive to target companies that already outsource their IT department versus prospects that are opposed to outsourcing. In this scenario, the current state detail of "currently outsourcing" is a key detail to add to the characteristics of our ideal prospect.

On the other side of that example, depending on your strategy and your product set, you may want to target businesses that do not already use what you sell. For example, if we sell automation software, you may want to search out prospects that have not automated a particular area yet. In this case, the characteristic of "manual processes" may be included in the current state characteristics of our ideal prospect.

BUILDING THE ATTACK LIST

Once you know what your ideal prospect looks like, you can take those characteristics and begin to build the target list of prospects for the area where you will focus your cold calling time and effort. A good first step is to perform a brainstorm session of all of the ideal prospects that you know about or already have a relationship with. This can be your warm list and the starting point for your activities.

Once you have gone through or have identified your warm prospects, you can build a large list of cold prospects. There are many different resources to use to build this list. First, you may have an internal database of contacts at your company that has collected contacts over the years. And if you do not, there are many external resources available where you can provide a list of ideal prospect details and get a long list of target prospects.

One example of an external list resource is LeadFerret, a web-based service that allows you to easily enter your ideal prospect details into a search page and then you will be able to immediately see and download a long list of prospects. One of the great things about LeadFerret is that most contacts come with an email address, which is a little different from other contact list providers. The pricing is also very reasonable and straightforward as their model is one where you purchase points and then simply use a point for each contact that you download.

SECTION II

CORE CONCEPTS

5

QUALIFY

SCREENING PROSPECTS

*I'm as proud of what we don't do
as I am of what we do.*

Steve Jobs

As we discussed in Chapter 4, time is both limited and valuable. That being the case, it is critical that you do what you can to increase the amount of time that you spend with high quality prospects and decrease the time you spend with low quality prospects. High quality prospects are simply prospects that have a high probability of purchasing something and low quality prospects are on the other side of the spectrum—they have a low probability of moving forward. To help separate the high quality from the low, you can use a tactic of qualifying.

WHAT IS QUALIFYING?

Qualifying at its most basic level is assessing the prospect in two areas. First, how well does the prospect fit with what you have to offer. This fit refers to how well she matches up in terms of needing and being able to use what you have.

Qualifying does not stop there as you also need to determine how likely the prospect is to actually make a purchase. She could be a perfect fit from a need standpoint, but that does not mean that she is well positioned to move forward.

The majority of qualifying is performed by asking the prospect a variety of probing questions and this chapter will outline what you need to ask and look for.

WHY QUALIFYING IS IMPORTANT

Qualifying is maybe one of the most important areas to grasp when trying to improve sales results and here are some key reasons why.

1. Time is limited and valuable

The time that you have to work with during the week is limited as there is nothing that you can do to add more hours to the day or week. As result, each hour that you have to work with is extremely valuable and in order to maximize your results, you must be effective at getting the most out of each hour. In order to protect the hours that you have to work with, you will want to maximize the time you spend with good, high quality prospects and minimize the time you spend with low quality prospects and qualifying will help with all of this.

2. Control is limited

Another factor that works against you is that your control over what prospects do is somewhat limited. You cannot control the prospects that you pursue – you cannot make him answer your call, call you back, or agree to make the purchase.

And while you can't control the prospects that you try to sell to, you can control <u>which</u> prospects that you try to sell to. In other words, you can control how selective you are over the prospects that you chose to spend your valuable time with and by being more selective and filling your time with high quality prospects, you will improve your ability to control prospects and sales opportunities.

3. Makes the call more conversational

By adding a qualifying step to your cold call, you will be asking the prospect questions and this will create an exchange of information. This can make a cold call more conversational compared to one where a sales person does all of the talking. When the call becomes more conversational, it will sound less like a cold call, and this can help to lower the prospect's guard.

When the call is more conversational, it will also help to get the prospect talking. This can greatly improve cold calls by keeping you from doing all of the talking. Not only will this allow you to gather more information, it will also draw the prospect in and make them more involved in the conversation, which can have a positive impact on the flow and length of the call.

4. Provides an opportunity to uncover pain

As you gather more information by asking some qualifying questions, it is possible that you may uncover some pain that the prospect is experiencing. We will discuss pain in more detail in Chapter 9, but finding pain during a cold call is a key step that can lead to success, and qualifying the prospect could be a good opportunity to uncover this type of valuable information.

5. Creates a better quality of leads

The goal of the cold call can differ from call to call, but it is very likely that you are trying to produce leads. And if you are working to produce leads, you will want those leads to be as good as they can be in terms of quality. If you ask qualifying questions during the cold call, you will be screening the prospect more, and this will filter out any leads that do not have a decent probability of moving forward. Having a better quality group of leads to work on can have tremendous benefits, as it can help with your pipeline and deal management, forecasting, and your close rate.

5. Fosters better relationships

In sales, building good relationships is key. When you qualify prospects, you position yourself to build better relationships. This can result due to a couple of factors. First, you will stand to make a better impression when qualifying as the prospect will observe you asking very polished and thorough questions. This positive impression could lead to the prospect respecting you more and being more open to working with you.

Another factor at play is that, when you go through the motions of trying to qualify the prospect, you can stand to decrease the prospect's guard as you will present yourself as making sure he is a fit before you sell to him. This will give off the impression that you are putting his best interest of making a good purchase ahead of your primary interest of closing a deal and this can help you to present yourself as a trusted advisor and this can fuel the level of rapport that you have with the prospect.

IDENTIFYING QUALIFIED PROSPECTS

In order to effectively qualify prospects, it can help to figure out exactly what to look for. To help with this, let's begin by comparing what a qualified prospect looks like compared to an unqualified prospect.

Qualified Prospect Characteristics

A common initial thought may be that you need to focus on prospects who have a high level of interest. But in reality, a truly qualified prospect requires more than just interest alone. For example, many people would love to have a Ferrari. If we had the opportunity, many of us would probably even take time out of our busy schedules to go test drive one just to see what it is like. In this scenario, we are very interested prospects, but are we qualified prospects? The answer is that we are not and this could be due to a deficiency in any one of four key qualification areas:

1. Need to purchase
2. Authority to purchase
3. Ability to purchase 4. Intent to purchase

1. Need to purchase

When trying to fight day in and day out to sell your products, it can be very refreshing to find a prospect that expresses interest in what you have to offer. But does a prospect showing interest "want" your products or does she "need" them? This can make a big difference when qualifying prospects. If it is more of a want than a need, the opportunity may get hung up at the end of the sales cycle when it is time for the prospect to pull the trigger on the transaction.

An example where a prospect might not have a true need is where you have discussions going and a prospect likes some of your features and is fairly interested. But the current system that the prospect is using is working OK. You could clearly improve things, but since things are OK and there are not any real problems or disruptions, there is not enough of a case to justify spending time, money, and energy to purchase from you. As a result, you could find yourself struggling to close the deal at the end of the sales cycle.

2. Authority to purchase

When you are dealing with a prospect, it can help to identify whether he has the authority to purchase from a decision making standpoint. In the example of the Ferrari, even if you take the extremely high price out of the equation, the prospect test driving the car might not have the authority to purchase as it could be a scenario where the spouse of the prospect is the one who decides what purchases get approved and made. In this case, regardless of how good of a job the sales person does, the prospect is not completely qualified until the person with the authority to purchase is involved in the process.

In business-to-business sales, many instances occur where individuals lower in the organization are responsible for interacting with vendors, and these individuals will likely not have the authority to purchase and sign off on larger transactions. When you are trying to qualify prospects, you need to understand what their level of decision-making power is and how they fit in the organization. This is not to say that you should not spend time with prospects that do not have the authority to make a purchase. What it does say is that you should not label extremely interested prospects that do not have decision-making power as qualified and you should be protective of the amount of time you spend with them until the individuals with the authority to purchase are involved in some way or another.

3. Ability to purchase

It can also help to identify whether the prospect has the ability to purchase from a budget or funding standpoint. If the person test driving the Ferrari is the decision-maker and has the authority to purchase, he still might not have the ability to purchase from not having enough money to spend and this will decrease the level of qualification.

When qualifying prospects, it can help to determine their ability to purchase in terms of available budget and funding. When qualifying the prospect's ability to purchase, not only is it important to identify whether there is funding available for the purchase, but we can also try to identify if there are other projects that could be competing for those funds and what process the prospect will have to go through to get funds approved and allocated.

4. Intent to purchase

The last thing to look at is whether or not the prospect has a genuine intent to purchase. If the prospect is strong in the areas of need, authority, and ability to purchase but does not intend to move forward with a purchase, the prospect is not completely qualified.

There are two scenarios where a prospect may spend time talking with you but not really intend to do anything. The first is when a prospect has interest, but he is not serious about making a purchase. "Window shopping" is a common term for this and the example of test driving for entertainment is a good example of a prospect that does not have genuine intent to purchase. This happens in the business world where prospects without genuine intent to purchase have sales people provide presentations, demonstrations, and proposals.

Another case where a prospect may have low intent to purchase is one where he has plans to purchase, but does not have plans to purchase from you. A very common example of this is where a prospect has spent the majority of the sales cycle talking with another vendor and reaching out to you at a very late stage in the process. A reason this may occur is that the prospect is primarily reaching out to you to just get another price to help assess and negotiate with the vendor that he plans on purchasing from.

In both of these cases, if the low level of intent to purchase goes undetected, the sales person stands to waste valuable time on a prospect that has very low probability of purchasing anything.

2-STEP QUALIFYING PROCESS

Hopefully by now you can see how important it is to screen and qualify prospects. Now let's get into how to effectively do that.

We provide you with a 2-step qualifying process. Step 1 is called soft qualifying and takes place primarily during a cold call or the first contact with the prospect. When you meet with the prospect in the first conversation or first meeting, you can move on to step 2 which is hard qualifying.

Soft Qualifying

Soft qualifying is focused primarily on determining whether it makes sense to meet and keep talking. In order to do this, you can ask a few questions to check out if the prospect has any open needs where you have something to offer, if the prospect is happy with the way things are going, and if you are talking to the right person. If you don't get the answers that you are looking for in those areas, you may reach a conclusion that it would not be a good use of anybody's time continuing to talk or scheduling a meeting.

Here are three key areas where you can spend some attention when soft qualifying:

1. Current state details

It can help to better understand the current state on the prospect's side in the area that your products or services impact. This basically involves finding out what the prospect is doing today and can include areas like processes, systems, people, vendors, etc. For example, if we sell email marketing software, we may want to find out if a prospect is doing email marketing today and if so, we will want to find out what tools they are using. Asking a couple of questions to grab those details is what we do to identify what the current state looks like.

Identifying what the prospect is doing today will provide tremendous information to help you to determine if it makes sense to keep talking at all. For example, if the prospect just signed a contract or recently invested heavily in a system that fills the needs that you want to talk to her about, it might not make sense for you to invest your valuable time in a first conversation, since the prospect is locked up and taken care of right now. On the other extreme, a question about the current state may reveal that the prospect has a tremendous need for change due to using outdated systems or manual processes.

The questions that you ask to gather current state details will be fairly dependent on your particular product, but they will basically probe for what is going on and what is being used. Here are three example current state questions that a sales person could ask:

"What are you currently using to detect security breaches?"

"When did you implement that system?"

"Are you locked into a contract with your current provider?"

Below is an outline of how to assess the information and answers you receive from the prospect:

- **Strong:** The prospect is not doing or using anything
- **Medium:** The prospect's current contract is expiring soon
- **Weak:** The prospect recently bought something
- **Weak:** The prospect is locked into a long-term contract

2. Level of satisfaction

Once you identify what the prospect is doing in the area that your products or services impact, you can inquire about how things are going and what his level of satisfaction is. Your goal here is try to identify if things are great, things are OK, or things could be better. If things are great in the area where you are trying to impact, you might not have a productive first conversation as you might not be able to offer much value to the prospect. On the other side of that example, if you inquire about the prospect's level of satisfaction and uncover that things are just OK or could be better, it might make sense to keep talking as there could be a productive conversation around what is not working well and how you can help.

The questions that you ask to gather level of satisfaction details will also be fairly dependent on your particular product, but they will basically probe for how the prospect feels things are going. Here are three questions that a sales person could ask to measure the level of satisfaction:

"How do you feel about your ability to view the current performance of your IT infrastructure?"

"How do you feel about the level of service from your current provider?"

"Is there any functionality that you need that is not provided by your current system?"

Below is an outline of how to assess the information and answers you receive from the prospect:

- **Strong:** Things could be better
- **Medium:** Things are OK
- **Weak:** Things are great or good

3. Organizational details

When performing some soft qualifying, you may want to inquire if the prospect is in the right area of the organization for it to make sense to keep talking. When you get into hard qualifying, you will dig deeper to identify how much power and authority the prospect has. At this early stage, you just want to find out if the prospect falls in the general area that you are calling to discuss.

Here are three examples questions to gather some organizational details:

"Are you involved in the management of the supply chain?"

"Is this an area that falls under your responsibility?"

"Is this an area that impacts you at all?"

Below is an outline of how to assess the information and answers you receive from the prospect:

- **Strong:** The prospect is the key person that oversees the area that your product impacts
- **Medium:** The prospect is in the area that your product impacts but at a lower level
- **Weak:** The prospect has nothing to do with the area that your product impacts

If you ask the prospect one to two questions from those three soft qualifying areas, you should be able to arrive at a point where you know if it makes sense for you to spend your valuable time talking more or meeting with the prospect.

Hard Qualifying

Once you progress to the first conversation stage of the sales cycle and beyond, you can begin to perform much harder qualifying to ensure that the prospect is worth spending valuable time on. For example, if a prospect wants us to show a demo or spend hours putting together a proposal, you will definitely want to ask some hard qualifying questions to make sure he is a qualified prospect before investing that time.

Hard qualifying focuses on assessing how the prospect fits across the four qualified prospect characteristics:

1. Need to purchase
2. Authority to purchase
3. Ability to purchase
4. Intent to purchase

1. Need to purchase

Once you get some formal time to meet with the prospect, try to dig deeper to really identify if the prospect has a true needs for what you have or if it is more of a "want".

Here are some questions that you can ask to assess the prospect's need to purchase:

"What happens if you do not make this purchase?"

"What improvements will you see if you move forward with this purchase?"

"Is there at date when this purchase needs to be made? What happens if the purchase is not made by that date?"

"What is the time frame that the project needs to work along?"

Below is an outline of how to assess the information and answers you receive from the prospect:

- **Strong:** Noticeable negative impact if there is no purchase
- **Strong:** Prospect needs to purchase something by a certain date
- **Medium:** Noticeable positive impact with purchase
- **Weak:** Can keep doing OK without a purchase

2. Authority to purchase

Once you feel like there is a real need on the prospect's side, you can begin to identify how much power and authority the prospect has. Here are some questions that you can ask to assess the prospect's authority to purchase:

"What is the decision making process?"

"What parties will be involved in making the decision?"

"What functional areas (departments) will be impacted by the purchase?"

"Who is the ultimate decision maker?"

"Who is the person that will need to sign the agreement/contract?"

Below is an outline of how to assess the information and answers you receive from the prospect:

- **Strong:** The prospect is the only person needed to approve the purchase
- **Medium:** Prospect makes the decision but has to get approval
- **Weak:** Prospect does not make final decision

3. Ability to purchase

As you progress through your hard qualifying, assess the prospect's ability to purchase. Here are some questions that you can ask to assess the prospect's ability to purchase:

"Is there a budget approved for this project?"

"What is the budget range that the project needs to fit in?"

"Have the funds been allocated to this purchase?"

"What budget (department) will this purchase be made under?"

"Are there other purchases that this funding may end up being used for?"

"How does the project fit with other initiatives from a priority standpoint?"

Below is an outline of how to assess the information and answers you receive from the prospect:

- **Strong:** Funds are available, approved, and allocated
- **Medium:** Funds are available but will need to be approved
- **Weak:** Funds are not available

4. Interest to purchase

The last thing to assess is how much genuine intent to purchase the prospect has. Here are some questions that you can ask:

"When are you looking to make this purchase?"

"What happens if you do not purchase anything?"

"Why did you contact us?"

"Why did you take time out of your schedule to meet with us?"

"What other options are you considering?"

"What other vendors are you looking at?"

"How far along are you with talking with them?"

"How do you feel about their solution?"

"What do you like about their solution?"

"What do you not like about their solution?"

"How does their solution compare with what we have to offer?"

"Is there a reason why you would choose us?"

"Is there anything that would prevent you from being able to choose us?"

"If you had to make a decision today, which way would you lean?"

Below is an outline of how to assess the information and answers you receive from the prospect:

- **Strong:** The prospect is serious about making a purchase
- **Strong:** The prospect is only talking with you
- **Medium:** The prospect is talking to other vendors but is favorable to your company
- **Weak:** The prospect sees all of the options as equal or leaning toward other options
- **Weak:** The prospect does not have definitive plans to purchase anything

Some Qualifying Questions Explained

We just provided a number of example qualifying questions and can't go through and explain why each one should be asked. But we would like to go through a few questions and explain why these questions are helpful and what the answers that you get from the prospect can mean.

Why do something?

When we are talking with a prospect and hear his needs, it can be easy for us to know why he should make a change and purchase from us. But does the prospect clearly know why it makes sense to make a change? One way to easily find out is to simply ask the prospect to answer "why do something" (or "why make a change")?

It can be tremendously powerful to ask the prospect why they should do something. If they are not sure or are not able to articulate why it makes sense, there can be some concern for the level of qualification of the prospect. If the prospect is qualified, he could respond to this question with an explanation of why it would make sense to move forward. Not only does this justify the continued investment of time, but you may also uncover new details around why the prospect needs your products during their explanation.

Why now?

If the purchase is a "must have," that is a good start toward the prospect being qualified. But is it a "must have" or is it a "must have right now"? Having the prospect answer the question of "why do something now" in their own words will help you to determine the time-line that the prospect is working against, and this will help you to determine how qualified he is.

You may find that the prospect has a compelling event approaching that will affect the timing of a purchase. A compelling event is an event or date that the purchase needs to be completed by. For example, if an existing agreement or contract is expiring on a specific date and the purchase will need to take place prior to that, that date is a compelling event. With such a date or event tied to the purchase, the prospect and lead becomes much more qualified. We might not know if the prospect is going to do business with *us*, but at least we know that there is a high probability that he is going to do something, and we know when he is likely to do it based on the compelling event. This is valuable information that we can use throughout the sales cycle while trying to manage meetings and deliverables with the prospect.

Why buy from us?

It is important to identify why the prospect would buy from us over the competition. We may know the answer, but having the prospect answer this question in his own words will give us tremendous information on how he perceives us compared to the competition. If the prospect cannot or will not communicate this to us, we may not be working with a qualified prospect.

What is the impact of doing nothing?

It is common for us to see our competition as the other companies against which we are competing for the prospect's business. But one of the biggest competitors that we face is the possibility of our prospect doing nothing and not making a purchase at all. In other words, the status quo can often be our biggest and most fierce competitor.

When qualifying, it is helpful to ask the prospect what happens if he does not make a change or go through with the purchase. If the answer reveals that there is not a huge impact or significant difference, then the prospect might not be qualified, as there might not be enough of a reason to make a change when it comes time to make the purchase.

Who else are you looking at?

To figure out how qualified the prospect is, it is very helpful to identify what other vendors the prospect is looking at. If we are the only vendor he is talking to, the prospect has a greater chance of purchasing from us, and this means that he is a more qualified prospect. If we are just one of many vendors he is looking at, the prospect is less qualified. If there are many vendors involved, this does not mean that we cannot win the business, but it could impact the amount of time that we invest and the expectations that we set in terms of forecasting the probability that we will secure the business.

How do you feel about your other options?

If we identify that the prospect is looking at other vendors, it can be very powerful to find out how he feels about the other options he is considering. When we hear who the competition is, we may have an initial thought about how we compare against those options and could fall into making assumptions about the prospect's perception. We could either think we are much better than his other options and consider the prospect to be very qualified. At the other extreme, we could hear the names of the competitors and think we don't have a shot and consider the prospect to not be qualified. But the reality is that the prospect's perception could be completely different from ours and it can be very helpful to identify how the prospect feels about the different directions he is considering.

How far along are you with the other vendors?

Once we identify the other vendors that the prospect is talking with, it is important to identify how far along in discussions the prospect is with them. If the prospect and other vendors are far along in terms of spending a significant amount of time together and having strong relationships already built up, we may be coming in at a very late stage. This could mean that we are at an extreme disadvantage to the other vendors, and as a result, the prospect might not be qualified.

Is the project budgeted?

It is important to identify whether the prospect has money to spend when trying to figure out how qualified he is. If he does not have money to spend, we should be careful with how much of our valuable time that we spend on him. While it can be uncomfortable to discuss money with a prospect, one easy way to bring it up and identify where the prospect is in terms of being able to make a purchase is to ask if the project or purchase has been budgeted. If the answer is "yes," then you know that there are funds available or allocated for the purchase, and this means the prospect is more qualified. If the answer is "no," this does not necessarily disqualify the prospect, but it can help you to determine the amount of priority and attention to give to it.

What size of budget are you trying to stay within?

Whether the purchase has been budgeted and has money available or not, we still can benefit from identifying how much money the prospect wants or expects to spend. If that expectation is not anywhere close to the area where our products and services are priced, then the prospect is not qualified and neither parties should invest too much time in the process.

It can sometimes be difficult to ask the prospect how much he wants or expects to spend because he will likely feel like we are crossing the line and getting into his business. In addition, he may feel like his answer will impact the pricing offered, so he either might not share any information or might share information that is not completely accurate. One way to try to identify what the prospect wants to spend is to ask what size of a budget he is trying to stay within.

What is the decision-making process?

It can be helpful to determine the level of purchasing power that the person we are dealing with has when trying to qualify the prospect. If the prospect has a high level of interest but does not have the authority to make a purchasing decision, the prospect is not qualified and we should be cautious how much time we spend working with him.

One easy way to determine how much purchasing power the prospect has is to simply ask what the decision-making process is for purchases and then map out the main steps of the process all the way to the point where a contract is signed. This map will tell us how much power the person we are dealing with has, as it will show how he fits into the organization. The more decision-making and purchasing power that prospect has, the more qualified the prospect is.

The answers to all of the qualifying questions that you ask will tell you a lot in terms of how qualified the prospect is. If a number of the answers that you receive are weak, that could mean that there is a low probability of the prospect moving forward when it is time to execute a purchase. With a low probability, you either need to go back and address the areas where the answers collected weren't as strong as you need them to be, or move on to find a more qualified prospect to spend your valuable time on.

6

OBJECTIONS

KEEPING CALLS GOING

I am a slow walker, but I never walk backwards.
ABRAHAM LINCOLN

There is one thing that can be guaranteed while cold calling, and that is that you will encounter objections on just about every call. Objections during a cold call are like stop signs that the prospect will hold up to try to take the call in a direction of her choosing. And if you have called someone unexpectedly and appear to possibly be trying to sell something, the direction of her choosing will likely be to bring the call to an end. Saying that she is not interested or not available are examples of how a prospect might use an objection to try to end our cold call.

But don't let the fact that you are sure to face objections discourage you. All you have to do to minimize this challenge is identify the objections that you anticipate running into and develop a strategy for how to get around them. By improving your level of preparedness for anticipated objections, you can see an immediate improvement in your ability to control cold calls and keep them going.

COMMON OBJECTIONS

One good thing about objections is that there are really only between five to ten objections that you will consistently face again and again while cold calling. Here are some examples of common objections:

"I do not have time right now."

"We are not interested."

"I am already using something for that."

"We do not have budget/money to spend right now."

"Call me back in six months."

"What is this in regards to?"

"He does not talk to vendors."

"Talk to my assistant."

"Just send me some information."

OBJECTIONS HANDLING OPTIONS

We have three main options for how to handle objections while cold calling.

Option 1 – Comply with the objection

One option when receiving an objection is to comply with it. This would be to give in to the objection and it will likely lead to the call slowing down and coming to an end. Below is an example:

Prospect: *"I am not interested."*

Caller: *"OK, sorry to bother you. Have a nice day."*

You will have to comply with some objections at some point, but when trying to drive results, it can help to not use compliance as your first response. A reasonable approach can be to try to deal with the objection in another way two to three times before complying.

Option 2 – Overcome the objection

Another option to pursue when faced with an objection is to try to overcome the objection. This would be to face the objection head-on and try to defuse it or to try to change the prospect's mind. Below is an example:

Prospect: *"I am not interested."*

Caller: *"OK, but we also have the auto tuning feature, and we are the global leader, with thirty years of experience."*

Trying to overcome an objection can be a less advantageous option for a couple of reasons. First, there is very little time to work with when you are talking to a prospect during a cold call. To address an objection head-on and try to overcome it would basically be trying to change someone's mind. This is a difficult task to take on, and a cold call simply does not provide the time and forum to be effective with this. If you receive an objection during a sales presentation or formal meeting, you will have more time and attention to work with and you will be able to be thorough as you build your case to overcome the objection and change the prospect's mind. But the environment is much faster and hostile on a cold call and it can be challenging to effectively and diplomatically build your case as to why you are right and the prospect is wrong.

Another reason that trying to overcome the objection can be a less advantageous path is that when you try to do so, you shine a spotlight on the objection by spending time discussing it. This can give it more life and energy, which can make it grow stronger and more grounded in the prospect's mind.

Option 3 – Redirect the objection

The third option for handling objections received when cold calling is to redirect the objection. This refers to trying to move the conversation into new territory or to keep the call going without addressing the objection head-on. Here is an example:

Prospect: *"I am not interested."*

Caller: *"I understand. Do you mind if I ask what you are doing today in to collect log data?"*

Prospect: *"We are using an in-house developed system."*

Redirecting essentially takes the call in a new direction. In the this example, by asking this question, the sales person moved the conversation away from the topic of the prospect not being interested and started a new, yet still related, conversation thread. If we continued moving forward with the example, it is reasonable for this conversation to continue in the redirected direction and begin to center around what the prospect is using today. The sales person might then have the opportunity to keep the conversation going by asking additional questions around what is working well and what is not working so well.

Note that if you actually reach a point where you redirect an objection and you arrive at a point where the prospect is sharing details around what is not working well, you have actually completely flipped a situation where the prospect went from trying to end your call to one where the prospect is sharing valuable information around their pain. (We will discuss pain more in Chapter 9.)

But whether you strike it rich with by having the prospect share some of their pain or not, the bottom line is that simply redirecting when a prospect throws an objection at you on a cold call can be a great tactic to keep the conversation going. And if you can improve your ability to keep calls going, you will improve the probability of consistently reaching the goal of transitioning to a first conversation.

RESPONDING TO COMMON OBJECTIONS

Here are examples of common objections, along with responses that have the potential to keep the calls moving forward.

I do not have time.

It is safe to assume that just about everybody you call is going to be busy—not only because prospects are at work, so they are likely working, but also because many people are doing the job of more than one person in today's business environment. In addition, if you are calling at a senior management level, not only do managers have very hectic schedules and heavy workloads, but they also have more pressure than ever from shareholders, economic conditions, compliance requirements, etc.

If you can assume that all prospects are busy, what needs to be determined is whether the prospect you reach is crazy busy or just normal busy. Crazy busy would be where the prospect is able to answer the phone but unavailable to talk due to being in the middle of a meeting, working on a deadline, or having some sort of high pressure emergency going on. Normal busy would be where the prospect is just dealing with the normal level of day-to-day busyness and possibly feels overwhelmed but that is something that is going on most of the day. Finding out whether the prospect is crazy or normal busy is important because you do not want to try to keep the calls going with crazy busy prospects as it will not be productive.

One way to respond to this objection and determine the prospect's level of busyness is to respond to the objection that she is busy with a response of, "I understand. I can be very brief or I can call back at another time." The prospect's response to this will usually be very telling. If she is crazy busy, she will not even entertain the thought of continuing and immediately push you to call back at another time. And this is good information and you can conclude that you have reached the prospect at a bad time to try to execute the cold call.

When you catch a prospect that is normal busy and you give her the option to talk now or for you to call back at another time, more often than not, she will tell you to go ahead and proceed in place of having you call back at another time. And if you move forward in this scenario, you know that she is busy but you are moving the conversation forward with her permission to continue, which buys you a little time to work with.

What is this in regards to?

This is one of the most common objections that gatekeepers and prospects use to screen calls. This question is designed to get the sales person to say something that signals that he is a sales person trying to sell something.

If you comply and directly answer this question, you might respond with a response that mentions that you are calling to introduce yourself, schedule a meeting, learn about their needs, etc. As soon as that type of response is delivered, a gatekeeper will immediately know that it is OK to shut you down and will do that with a response like, "Oh, we don't accept sales calls." From there, it is tough to recover and justify why it makes sense for you to keep going and the call will usually come to an end.

In order to avoid complying and falling into this common trap, you can redirect with a response that goes in a new direction and does not necessarily trigger sales person alerts. One approach that could do that is to answer with a version of your value statement. For example, you could deliver a response like, "The reason I am calling is that we help companies to reduce their cost of goods sold by 10 to 15 percent."

When you use a response like this, the gatekeeper or prospect will not hear the language from you that he is looking for and will actually be thrown off a little as he will be looking for words that point you out as a sales person. This is not to say that he will hear your value statement and completely open up and let you in. But his attempt to immediately shut you down can likely be stopped buying you a little more time.

The value statement also usually includes subjects that are more difficult to object to with responses about being not interested or not needing. For example, if your value statement talks about improving processes or costs, it is more difficult for a prospect to respond to you that he is not interested in improving processes or decreasing costs than it is for him to say that he is not interested in your products.

I do not have budget/money.

A common objection is for prospects to say that they do not have any budget or money available for your products. If this comes up on a cold call, it is really not a legitimate objection, as you are not trying to sell anything: your goal is simply to establish a first conversation. You can let them know this by saying, "I understand, and I want you to know that I am not trying to sell you anything, as I don't really know if what we have is a good fit for you." From there you can redirect to one of your soft qualifying questions to try to keep the cold call going.

I am not interested.

When a prospect says she is not interested, we can redirect to one of our soft qualifying questions. This lets us shift the focus away from her perceived lack of interest and redirect to a question that gets her talking about something else and keeps the call going. This could be accomplished by saying, "I understand. But if I could ask you real quickly, do you currently have a detection system in place?"

I am already using something today.

If the prospect tries to end the call with the objection that she is already using something for what we are calling about, you can redirect to get her to talk about what she is using. For example, you can respond with, "Oh I see. Do you mind if I ask what you are doing in this area?" From there, you can continue to inquire about what she is doing by asking what is working well and then trying to ask what is not working well. In many cases, this could help you to get around the objection and keep the call going. This direction will also possibly create a productive conversation where you are able to collect key details around the current state in terms of systems, processes, pain points, etc.

I am not looking to make a change right now.

If the prospect states that she is not looking to make a change right now, you can respond in a similar way to how you would respond if she objected by saying she does not have money or is not interested—by using a soft qualifying question. You can simply say, "I understand. And I want you to know that I am not calling you to sign you up for anything, as I don't really know if what we have is a fit for you all at this point. But if I could ask you a quick question, how long have you been using you current system?"

Just send me information.

One of the most common objections that gatekeepers and prospects will use to get rid of sales people is to ask the caller to send him some information. This is used a lot as it allows both gatekeepers and prospect to get rid of sales people quickly and effectively since it gives the sales person a little hint of hope that there might be interest. Another reason this is an objection that comes up a lot is that the person delivering it can get rid of the caller without looking rude and he can then just delete or throw away the information is sent over. The real frustrating thing about this objection is that it causes sales people to have false hope and waste time crafting follow-up messages.

Before we go further, it is important to note that this objection can actually occur at two different times during a cold call, and your response may differ according to when it comes up. If you get this early in the call, this is more of a blow-off objection, and you can reply by trying to redirect back to one of your soft qualifying questions. For example, you can reply with, "I can definitely send you some information. So that I know exactly what to send you, do you mind if I ask you what you are using for security monitoring?"

This objection can also come up later in cold call after some significant discussion, when you are trying to close. This situation is less of a blow-off scenario and more of one in which the prospect does not want to commit to moving forward. If you are at the end of the cold call, you might not be able to redirect back to any soft qualifying questions or to additional conversation threads. That being the case, one option that you have is to tell the prospect that you can send information, but to inquire about what he would like you to send and inquire why he would like you to send it. Does he want more information to get more educated so that he can make a decision? If so, you can redirect to the point that scheduling a conversation to answer questions would be much quicker and easier for him than you sending a bunch of information for him to read through on his own.

Remember—and I can't stress this enough—your goal is not to sell the prospect; it is to transition him into a first conversation. As a result, you can redirect to a response that reinforces the fact that you are not trying to sell her anything and are simply trying to establish open lines of communication between the two organizations. From there, you can redirect to questions that identify the prospect's level of interest, what his questions might be, what type of information he is looking for and why, and so on.

CREATE AN OBJECTIONS MAP

One way to improve your preparedness for objections is to create a tool that lists all of the objections that you could imagine being faced with and then script out responses that have the best chances of keeping the calls going. Once you have this list built, you could then use this as a map for where to go and what to do when objections come up while cold calling. The following is an example of an objections map.

Objection	Response
I am busy.	I understand. I can be very brief or I can call back at another time.
What is this call in regards to?	The purpose for my call is that [insert value statement].
I do not have budget/money.	I understand, and I want you to know that I am not trying to sell you anything, as I don't really know if what we have is a good fit for you. (Redirect) But if I could ask you real quickly, [insert soft qualifying question].
I am not interested.	I understand, and I want you to know that I am not trying to sell you anything, as I don't really know if what we have is a good fit for you. (Redirect) But if I could ask you real quickly, [insert soft qualifying question].
I am already using something today.	Oh I see. Do you mind if I ask what you are doing in this area? How is it working? How long have you been doing that? What could be working better? (Redirect to soft qualifying question or typical pain points)
I am not looking to make a change right now.	I understand, and I want you to know that I am not trying to sell you anything as I don't really know if what we have is a good fit for you. (Redirect) But if I could ask you real quickly, [insert soft qualifying question].
Just send me information. (early in a call – blow off)	I can definitely send you some information. So that I know exactly what to send you, do you mind if I ask you [insert soft qualifying question].
Just send me information. (end of the call – noncommittal)	I can definitely send you some information. Do you mind if I ask what information you would like me to send? If you have questions, it might be quicker for you if we schedule a quick follow-up conversation versus sending you a bunch of information to read through.

The objections map should be a living and breathing document. As you encounter new objections, you should add those to the document and script out the best way to handle them. You can also continually evaluate your existing responses to identify whether they are working well to keep the calls going and explore other approaches that you could use to improve results.

7

DISQUALIFY

PUSHING AWAY
TO MOVE FORWARD

If they give you lined paper, write the other way.

WILLIAM CARLOS WILLIAMS

If we look at the natural roles of a sales person and a prospect, the sales person is typically the pursuer and the prospect is usually the pursued. And as part of that dynamic, the sales person usually communicates in a way that tries to promote, persuade, and push the prospect to move forward. While that approach is pretty much a requirement for a sales person to be successful most of the time, there can actually be some very powerful results when a sales person takes the completely opposite approach—taking away from the prospect the possibility of moving forward at very selective times.

This approach or tactic can be referred to as disqualifying the prospect, as it involves sharing with him that you question or doubt if he is the right fit for what you have to offer. Some people call this a "takeaway" tactic because you are basically taking away what you were originally trying to sell.

DISQUALIFYING EXPLAINED

In Chapter 5, we broke down the tactic of qualifying prospects. This is where you try to identify how well a prospect fits with what you have to offer in order to determine how likely he is to move forward with a purchase. If you went through a thorough qualifying process and determined that the prospect was not the right fit, you could reach a point of official disqualification of the prospect and completely shut the door on moving forward. The sales tactic of disqualifying is slightly less official than this, as you are really just bringing up the possibility of disqualification to the prospect to try to trigger some sort of reaction or action.

An example of disqualifying would be to say to a prospect who is on the fence or not showing a high level of interest, "Maybe this is not something you really need right now." When you say this reality-check type of statement, you are essentially testing the prospect's level of interest and qualification by doubting or questioning if it makes sense to continue. From this, you stand to trigger one of three potential reactions.

Potential Reaction #1 – No reaction

The possibility does exist that you disqualify a prospect and there is no reaction. This is not likely because a disqualifying statement is fairly bold and attention getting, but when considering all the possible outcomes, no reaction should be included.

Potential Reaction #2 – The prospect confirms the disqualification

It is important to know that the possibility does exist for the prospect to confirm the disqualifying questions, moving him to become definitively disqualified. Having this as a potential outcome may appear to add risk when using this tactic, but as long as you are using this tactic at the right time, this outcome will actually be a good thing.

If you fully disqualify a prospect and close the door on one who was not going to buy from you, you may have just saved yourself time that could have been wasted on trying to get him to move forward and preserving this time is a very good thing. Time is both limited and valuable, and in this scenario, you can then repurpose the saved time toward finding qualified prospects that have a high probability of moving forward.

What you don't want to do is disqualify prospects at the wrong time and create a negative reaction or official disqualification for a prospect who had a decent probability of moving forward. The key point here is that this is an advanced sales tactic and there is a specific time when you should disqualify. There is some logic provided later in this chapter that explains exactly when to disqualify.

Potential Reaction #3 – The prospect challenges the disqualification

The third potential reaction from disqualifying a prospect is that the prospect could challenge the disqualification attempt. An example of this would be if the prospect responds by challenging your doubt to explain why there is indeed a fit.

The powerful thing about this outcome is that when this happens, the prospect somewhat begins taking a role of selling to the sales person on why to keep moving forward. This may sound far-fetched or ambitious to have this type of exchange with a prospect, but if you have uncovered pain, built a level of rapport, and have triggered interest, then getting a prospect to confirm why it makes sense to move forward is a very realistic scenario.

FLIPPING THE TABLES

The interesting thing about this sales tactic is that you could not employ a more counterintuitive approach. You are a sales person and you need to find prospects and close deals, and you are going to tell a prospect that he isn't a good fit? And this is going to help you to increase sales? YES. This is a result of six powerful results that can occur when using the disqualifying tactic.

1. Improvement in level of rapport

When you disqualify a prospect, at that very moment we are likely doing the exact opposite of what the prospect would expect the typical sales person to do. Most sales people will aggressively try to sell. And when the prospect is on the fence or not showing interest, the average sales person will likely increase the level of aggressiveness and try harder. By not doing that and actually pushing the prospect away, you will not only stand out from the majority of other sales people, but you will also display qualities such as confidence, integrity, humility, intelligence, directness, etc. When a prospect sees these characteristics all at once, you are likely to see a significant spike in the level of rapport that you have with him.

2. Improvement in credibility

Similar to the spike in rapport, you are likely to see an increase in your credibility when you disqualify a prospect. This is because at the exact moment that you disqualify the prospect, you are talking about what is best for him instead of what is best for you. If one of your top goals is to close sales, and you display that you are putting the prospect's best interest of making a good decision in front of that, there will be an immediate display of integrity. When you are able to display integrity and honesty to the prospect, you can often create an implied effect that you must also be using integrity and honesty when you are talking about your company and all of the great things that your products and services do.

3. Improvement in quality of leads

As we saw from Potential Reaction #2, the prospect can confirm your disqualification and that could result in him going away. While that could appear to be a bad outcome, if he was never going to buy from us, it is actually a very good outcome to have him go away. The result of this is that you just removed a low-quality lead from your pipeline, and this can help to clean up the active leads that you are tracking and working, which can improve your ability to build sales forecasts, improve your close rate, and free up time to find new prospects.

4. Improvement in deal momentum

When working with prospects who are on the fence and not wanting to move in any direction, this tactic can often trigger some sort of action and get these prospects off of the fence and instigate forward movement that might not have occurred otherwise.

5. Uncover new information

If the reaction that you get from disqualifying a prospect is that he challenges the disqualification, be sure to listen closely during this powerful moment. Not only do you want to listen to see if the prospect confirms being on the same page with us, but also listen closely as the prospect may share new information for why he is interested or why he feels there is a strong fit between his needs and what you have to offer.

An example of this might be where you have identified two problems that your product will solve for the prospect. If you were uncertain about what the prospect was thinking and disqualified him, he may respond by confirming the two problems that you had in mind and then share one more very important problem that you will solve that you were not originally aware of. Identifying that additional problem that you solve is valuable information and you can use this as you continue to build your business case and work to close the deal.

6. Improvement in close rate

The byproduct from all of these improvements can be an improvement in the overall close rate. If you are positively impacting any of the areas of rapport, credibility, quality of pipeline, deal momentum, and uncovering new information, it is very safe to assume that you could see an improvement in your ability to close.

WHEN TO DISQUALIFY

It is important to point out that disqualifying is an advanced sales tactic and it is critical to use it at the right time. In order to clearly explain when to disqualify, let's outline three potential temperatures or positions for the prospects we deal with.

Position #1 – Positive: This is where the prospect is displaying a high level of interest in your products and services. This is displayed either verbally through direct statements confirming their interest, or through their actions, such as being very responsive, sharing information, and proactively instigating communications.

Position #2 – Neutral: The neutral position is one where the prospect could be described as indifferent or "on the fence." A neutral state will be visible when a prospect is not really showing interest in moving forward, but is also not shutting down the possibility of moving forward or communicating a lack of interest. This prospect might not be very responsive, but he is not completely unresponsive either. He is essentially in the middle—somewhere between interested and not interested.

Position #3 – Negative: A prospect in the negative position would be one who appears to be uninterested in what you are selling. This can usually be easily seen in fairly direct verbal communication—the prospect expresses a lack of interest in moving forward—or in behavior—the prospect is completely unresponsive to any attempts to communicate.

Once you have those three positions identified, it is fairly easy to identify when to use the tactic of disqualifying: It should only be used when prospects are in the neutral position. This is because you would never want to disqualify a prospect who is in a very positive position, as there is no need to. In that situation, you can just go with the positive momentum. You could disqualify when the prospect is in the negative position, but it might not have much of an effect, since you are essentially pushing away a prospect who is already moving away from you.

But if you have a prospect who is in an neutral position—he is indecisive, on the fence, and not sending clear signals—you can disqualify these prospects to try to trigger a reaction, and that could either pull them into the positive position or push them away into being confirmed in a negative position.

AN EXAMPLE PLAYED OUT

To look at a real-world example of this, let's take a situation that just about everybody can relate to: the act of someone looking to buy a new car. In this scenario, the prospect has been considering buying a car for some time, has done the research, has completed the test driving, and has narrowed the choice to one car. She has expressed interest but is hesitant to move forward to the next step in the process, which is to execute the purchase.

At this point, the momentum and speed of the sales cycle has slowed, and the prospect is clearly in a neutral position. She started out very positive in terms of interest, but as we progressed through the sales cycle, she has slowed and become indecisive. It is important to point out that she is very qualified in terms of needing to make a purchase because her current vehicle is unreliable, she has the ability to purchase from a budget standpoint, she has the authority to purchase, as she is the decision maker, and she has genuine intent to purchase.

Our time is valuable, and time kills deals, so there are a few options that we have in order to try to trigger some movement:

Option 1 – Do nothing: We could do nothing and let the prospect manage the speed and direction. This can lead to getting stuck in "idle land," which could result in more time being wasted on both sides and increase the probability of "no decision."

Option 2 – Become more aggressive: We could try to sell more aggressively to the prospect by going back to talk more about all of the features and benefits. The risk here is that if there is internal conflict going on for the prospect, then by pushing harder, we could end up pushing her away.

Option 3 – Disqualify: When we notice the hesitation and internal conflict, we can disqualify by mentioning that maybe the purchase is not right. After this statement of doubt is made, if the purchase is genuinely a good fit, the prospect might challenge the disqualification and share with us why it makes sense to move forward. But if it is ultimately not a good fit, the prospect may confirm the disqualification and end up going away.

As you can see from those options, disqualifying a prospect when she shows indifference or hesitation can be a very powerful sales tactic to try to trigger some action. It does come at a risk, but as explained, if we disqualify at the right time and the prospect does not have a good chance of moving forward, the outcome of the prospect going away can be a positive scenario.

SOFT DISQUALIFYING

Similar to soft qualifying, you can perform some soft disqualifying during a cold call to trigger some positive reactions. This could involve a statement very early in the call that questions whether the prospect is a good fit. For example, after you introduce yourself and share some sort of value statement, you could say "I actually don't know if what we have will fit well with you or not" or "I am not sure if you are the right person to speak with or not". From there, you can continue forward with your script and transition to a few soft qualifying questions.

When you use a soft disqualifying statement early in a call, it can help to decrease the prospect's guard as you will present yourself as a "not so aggressive sales person" and that you are keeping the prospect's best interest in mind. You also might create a little curiosity on the prospect's side because you are slightly taking away what you have to offer and presenting yourself as having something of value. This can be a great, nonthreatening way to begin a cold call.

DISQUALIFYING DISCLAIMER

It is also important to point out that this tactic is designed more for professional business-to-business sales where relationships and "win/win" transactions are very important. In some business-to-consumer sales scenarios, closing transactions through pressure and capitalizing on prospect impulsiveness is a key to success. In those scenarios, you could still use a flavor of disqualifying but it may come with more of a risk and could be more delicate to incorporate.

Returning to the example of new car sales, this is actually a profession in which overuse of the disqualifying tactic could have a fairly negative impact on the sales person and the dealership. While you could say that you should not sell a car to someone who is not 100 percent comfortable with the decision, the auto industry thrives on somewhat impulsive decisions. No disrespect to sales professionals or buyers in that industry is intended—it is just a fact that auto purchases are big-ticket items for consumers and there is always a little doubt and hesitation, so if you bring too much rational thinking to the process, there could sometimes be a negative impact on sales results.

Corporate or business-to-business sales utilize a more thorough and formal purchasing process, allowing you to push back on prospects at certain times. And you definitely would not want to pressure a business to spend millions of dollars on a purchase if it is not completely the right fit.

8

GATEKEEPER

TURNING AN
ENEMY INTO AN ALLY

Seek to understand in order to be understood.

STEPHEN COVEY

When making business-to-business cold calls, it is likely that you will have to face and go through many gatekeepers. This can be a frequent occurrence, as your target prospects will sometimes have their phones routed to a gatekeeper or you may only have a main number for a business. A gatekeeper is a receptionist or an executive assistant who answers your calls and stands between you and the person you want to talk with. Some gatekeepers will be very helpful and share information to help you get where you want to go. Some will not help much and will even appear like they are doing everything they can do to shut us down. Whatever the case, there are some very clear things that you can do while cold calling to improve your ability to turn gatekeepers from enemies into allies.

IMPORTANCE OF THIS VARIABLE

Depending on the prospects you are trying to reach, it could be reasonable to expect to spend up to 50 percent of your cold calling time interacting with gatekeepers. That being the case, figuring out how to operate a little better in this one area can have a pretty big and immediate impact on your cold calling results.

In addition, gatekeepers will typically have more knowledge and power than you might think. They not only usually have knowledge on processes and initiatives, but they can also sometimes have influence on decisions that are made. So not only do you want to find ways to get around gatekeepers, you should also to try to get them on your side and find ways to extract information.

TYPES OF GATEKEEPERS

There are a few different types of gatekeepers that you will face. It is worth breaking these down as they are fairly different from one another in terms of how they will treat you and also the knowledge that they usually have.

Front-Desk Receptionist

The front desk receptionist is the person that sits in the lobby of an office or headquarters of a business and will be responsible for checking in guests, receiving packages, and answering incoming calls. When you call a business' main number, you may be directed to a front-desk receptionist.

As we break down these different types of gatekeepers, we will outline three different areas that you should keep in mind: work environment, level of knowledge, and focus on screening.

Work Environment: The front-desk receptionists are one of the busier gatekeepers that you will face. This is because they usually have a steady flow of requests. Whether it is someone walking up or the phone ringing, there is typically always something to deal with and it can often be like that all day long.

What this means is that you will not be able to get much attention and time from front-desk receptionists and you may notice this from them putting you on hold and rush to get off the phone when you try to talk for any length of time. It is also this environment that can feed into these gatekeepers sometimes being ugly and unhelpful. They are extremely busy and have been dealing with nonstop requests all day and many of those are from other sales people like you that are trying to get in.

Level of Knowledge: Since front-desk receptionists are constantly directing guests and routing calls, they can often have a decent level of knowledge of the organizational structure and who does what. Although, this knowledge will be somewhat limited to titles and departments and they will likely not have in-depth knowledge about what an individual does or is responsible for.

Focus on Screening: This type of gatekeepers will often have a high focus on screening out sales calls as it is often part of their assigned responsibilities. These gatekeepers have often received training and instruction on how to best do block sales calls.

Switchboard Operators

Switchboard operators are similar to the front-desk receptionists in that they will answer a business' main phone number, but that is all that they do. Instead of sitting in the lobby of an office, these gatekeepers are usually operating in a back office somewhere and just focused on routing calls.

Work Environment: Switchboard operators have a little less going on than front-desk receptionists, so it is a little less of a chaotic environment making them little more available to talk to.

Level of Knowledge: Unfortunately, while these gatekeepers are a little more available, they will typically not have very much organizational knowledge and will usually only be able to answer questions with the information that is displayed in the systems and directory that they have access.

Focus on Screening: Switchboard operators will be less likely to try to screen you out as their job is to connect you with who you are trying to reach.

Executive Assistants

Executive assistants are individuals that are in an administrative role and typically support a few executives and sometimes also the department that the executive presides over. Executive assistants often answer the phone for the executives that they support, and when you cold call at that level, you can definitely expect to interact with this type of gatekeeper.

Work Environment: The environment that an executive assistant works in can be somewhat chaotic with supporting a large number of people, but usually not as bad as what a front-desk receptionist is in. Why this is relevant to you is that you can likely talk to this type of gatekeeper for few minutes without causing a major disruption and being rushed to get off the phone.

Level of Knowledge: The other key detail with executive assistants is that they usually have extensive knowledge of the organization, business details, current processes and systems, challenges, and initiatives. They have this knowledge because they are simply exposed to it as they work closely with the executives and departments. This makes this type of gatekeeper a great resource for information. They also can often have some level of power and influence so it can be good to stay on their good side.

Focus on Screening: Just like any other gatekeeper, the executive assistant will be cognizant of the need to perform some level of screening to prevent just letting everybody through. But one good thing about these gatekeepers is that they can be a little more professional in how they screen you. Instead of just giving you objection after objection and trying to block out anybody that appears to be selling something, an executive assistant may ask you some questions to try to learn more about you in order to make a more informed decision for whether or not to let you in.

Automated Attendants

Automated attendants are the recorded menu trees that answer your call in place of a live person. While these are not a physical person, they are definitely a gatekeeper that will stand between you and the prospect that you want to talk to.

With the cost savings associated, and advancements in the underlying technology, automated attendants are becoming increasingly more common, especially when calling into large businesses. That is actually not very good news as these can be one of the more difficult gatekeepers that you will face as they can be extremely time consuming and difficult to navigate.

UNDERSTANDING THE GATEKEEPER

The first step in improving your ability to work with gatekeepers is to improve your understanding of them. As Dr. Stephen Covey writes in *The 7 Habits of Highly Effective People*, you can improve relationships by "seeking to understand in order to be understood." This powerful concept is based on the principle that you can build stronger relationships and become better understood by others if you first make an effort to understand them.

Applying this to dealing with gatekeepers, we definitely want to be understood by them, as we want them to understand why it makes sense to let us in. In order to help create that scenario, you can begin by understanding the gatekeeper and the world he lives in.

A Day in the Life

Whether the gatekeeper is a receptionist for an entire office or an executive assistant for a few individuals, his day is typically very hectic. And while everybody may have a hectic day in some way or another, a gatekeeper's hectic activity will include a barrage of incoming calls all day. In addition to fielding calls, he will probably have to respond to and balance a constant flow of in-person requests from visitors and employees.

When your call and is answered by a gatekeeper, it is likely part of this barrage. Not only are you one of many calls that the gatekeeper will have to field while performing other duties, you will likely be one of many sales people who are cold calling to try to get into the company.

By being empathic to what the environment on the other end of the phone is like, you can begin to improve your ability to understand and deal with the gatekeeper.

The Gatekeeper's Main Objective

Now that we realize how chaotic the workday can be for gatekeepers, we need to stop to think about one of the main objectives that they have been assigned. By understanding what the gatekeeper is trying to accomplish, you can instantly improve your ability to understand, appreciate, and anticipate his actions and reactions.

Unfortunately, most prospects do not want to receive cold calls, and in an attempt to eliminate or minimize having to deal with them, it is very common for target prospects to assign gatekeepers with a clear objective of keeping out unsolicited sales calls. You can usually tell when a gatekeeper has been assigned this task, as he will typically ask a lot of questions, not give out any information, and can sometimes be difficult. In many cases, just as sales people use sales training to learn tactics to get into accounts, gatekeepers will be trained on using certain tactics to keep sales people out.

What is helpful to be aware of here is that when gatekeepers are being difficult and clearly trying to screen you out, they are really just trying to do their job and meet the objective they have been given. When this is the case, the harder you try to get in, the harder they may try to keep you out. A natural reaction to this might be to get mad and take personally the fact that they are not being nice and not helping you out. But when you understand and appreciate where they are coming from, you can begin to figure out how to work with them so that you can work together to both be successful.

GATEKEEPER TACTICS

There are a few very clear and simple things that you can do to improve your ability to build relationships with gatekeepers and turn them from enemies to allies.

Befriend

It is not rocket science to figure out that you can work better with gate-keepers when you are able to establish more friendly interactions and relationships with them. But what can you do to improve your ability to build relationships and seem more likeable to them?

> *Use the gatekeeper's name:* One minor tactic to use to create a more personal conversation and create a slightly tighter bond with gatekeepers is to simply catch or ask for their name and use it often when talking with them. You can take this one step further by actually making a note on your side of the gatekeeper's name so that you can use the name again when we call back, picking up where you left of in terms of creating rapport.

> *Use of tonality:* The subject of tonality is discussed more in Chapter 16, but your voice has a large impact on how people receive you over the phone, and there are some minor things you can do in that area to improve your gatekeeper relations. One thing that you can easily do is to smile when making calls – "smile and dial". This can modify the friendliness and warmth of your voice, and this minor change could improve a gatekeeper's willingness to help.

Try to Enlist Their Help

Another tactic to improve your interactions with gatekeepers is to try to enlist their help to get you going in the right direction. This can be accomplished indirectly by talking with a tonality that is a mix of curious and a little lost. If you can add question marks to your statements and speak with a more puzzled face, you can create more of a lost tone in your voice, and this can be a way of encouraging the gatekeeper to want to be on our side, to want to help you.

You can also very directly ask for their help. For example, by simply changing, "Can you please connect me with the training manager?" to something like, "I am trying to connect with the manager of training? Can you help point me in the right direction?" you are presenting yourself as more vulnerable and in need of help, and this could have a positive impact on the interaction with the gatekeeper.

Establish Social Proof

When the gatekeeper answers your call, if he is assigned the task of keeping sales people out, he will likely be trying to determine if you are a friend or a foe. A friend is somebody that the company already knows, someone who is in some way or another on the inside. And a foe is someone on the outside trying to get in. Sales people who are cold calling are most likely going to fall into the foe category.

One way to quickly try to prevent the gatekeeper from thinking that you are a foe is to establish social proof and there are two quick and effective ways to establish social proof.

1. Name Dropping

Name dropping will be discussed in more detail in Chapter 12, but it is a concept where you present yourself as already being connected with the gatekeeper's organization and do this by sharing names of individuals in the organization with whom you have met with. When you do this, the gatekeeper will immediately have the impression that you are already somewhat on the inside and will be more comfortable passing you through or helping out. Here is an example what this could look like:

"Well, we met last week with Marcus Stone in accounting and now I am trying to connect with the person that oversees HR. Can you point me in the right direction of whom I should talk to?"

You might be thinking to yourself, that is all great, but what if we have not met or spoken with anybody? Well, one way to still use name dropping in that scenario is to simply name drop individuals in the organization that we are planning on calling or meeting with. When said the right way, you can establish a sense of already being on the inside, even when you have not spoken to anyone. Here is an example of what that looks like:

"Well, we are planning on meeting with Tina Martinez next month, but we are trying to connect with an operations manager prior to that. Can you help point me in the right direction of whom that might be?"

You may think that this is being misleading to mention that we are planning on meeting with Tina Martinez, when we have not talked with her yet. But the key word here is that we are "planning" on meeting with Tina. If everything goes right, hopefully we will be meeting with Ms. Martinez in the near future, making that 100% our plans and our statement honest and fairly accurate.

2. Mention an Initiative

You can also create social proof by mentioning that you are calling to schedule a meeting to discuss a particular initiative. This will add to your credibility and make you appear to be on the inside, since you are knowledgeable about current initiatives. You may have to do some homework in order to identify an initiative that can be referenced. But if you do not have one to mention, there are some initiatives that are fairly generic and which just about every company has, like initiatives to decrease costs, improve processes, increase compliance, increase revenue, etc.

Treat the Gatekeeper like a Prospect

When you face a gatekeeper that is being extremely resistant to helping or is unclear as to where to send you, it can sometimes help to take a step back and treat the gatekeeper like the target prospect. This involves sharing more information about who you are and why you are calling.

A good time to use this tactic is when you feel like you have hit a brick wall and are struggling to get any progress with the gatekeeper. When that is the case, it may be time to say something like this:

"Actually, maybe it might make sense if I take a step back and tell you who I am and why I am calling. My name is Nancy Flinn and I am with a company that helps businesses like yours to better manage their vendor agreements. A lot of our clients came over to us because they were paying unnecessary contract fees. I don't know if you all are experiencing the same challenges and that is why I am trying to connect with the person on your side in charge of managing vendor relationships. Can you help to point me in the right direction?"

In that example, we might have started out the beginning of the call just trying to get right through to the target prospect, but once we noticed a little difficulty, we stopped and shared more information with the gatekeeper. The information shared in the example was a value statement and a common pain point that our ideal prospects typically face.

Not only can treating a gatekeeper like a prospect help to get him to understand why it makes sense to let you through, it can also sometimes help him to figure out where it makes the most sense for you to go. In addition, the gatekeeper can sometimes have a tremendous amount of knowledge on the organization and current state, and this can be a good opportunity to try to extract some valuable information from him.

Ask Qualifying Questions

Another tactic to use, and one that also treats the gatekeeper like a prospect, is the tactic of asking the gatekeeper the qualifying questions that you have prepared for the target prospect. The time to employ this tactic is when you feel like you are starting to get blocked out. The gatekeeper won't let you in – fine, start asking the gatekeeper the key questions that you had ready for the target prospect.

Here is an example of what this could look like when a gatekeeper says that they are not interested:

"I understand. If I could ask you real quick, do you know if your maintenance management software was developed in-house or did you all invest in a commercial application?"

When you ask this type of question, you are redirecting away from the gatekeeper's objection and over to a new area of discussion and this can help you to keep the call going. And who knows, you may end up getting some valuable information if the gatekeeper is able to answer some of your questions.

Another reason to use this tactic is that you may end up asking questions that he does not know the answers to. When that happens, not only does it weaken their power to say "no", but it also creates a reason for why it makes sense for you to talk to the target prospect. To take advantage of this opportunity, you can respond with something like this when the gatekeeper shows an inability to answer your questions:

"Oh I see. Well, that is why we are trying to connect with the operations manager. Do you know who would be the right person to ask about that?"

An ideal time to use this is when the gatekeeper is giving you the objection that the company does not need what you have or that they are not interested.

Share that You Understand

At some points, you may feel like you are in a stalemate with the gatekeeper. You are trying your hardest to get in and he is trying his hardest to keep you out. One tactic to use here is to call a spade a spade by telling the gatekeeper that you understand where he is coming from. This approach could include you sharing that you know that his job is hectic, that he gets a lot of sales people calling all day long, and possibly share that you know that he has been assigned the objective of trying to keep out some of the calls that appear to be sales calls.

It is very important to use a warm and friendly tone when using this tactic. If you are not diplomatic and use the right tonality and finesse, you could possibly create a confrontational moment taking a step backwards. An easy way to see this is, if you are smiling as you share this, you can create a positive reaction. But if you are very serious, and have a frustrated face and tone, it will push you and the gatekeeper apart.

One of the reasons this can help is that, by sharing with the gatekeeper that you understand his situation, you a feeding one of his internal needs to be understood. When you are at odds with a gatekeeper and he is doing everything he can to keep you out and you are able to share with him that you understand where he is coming from, it is very possible for him to begin to decrease his guard a little.

If you are able to create this type of shift, you can then use the previously discussed tactic of treating the gatekeeper like a prospect and begin to share with him how you help other businesses and ask a few questions. From there, you can possibly gather some valuable information from him and sell him on why it makes sense to let you in. After that type of exchange, not only might he let you in, but he might be very helpful in sharing where you need to go and whom you need to talk to.

Avoiding the Gatekeeper Altogether

One tactic to mix in is to adjust your prospecting so that you avoid having to deal with gatekeepers altogether. A good way to do this is to call when they are likely to not be around. Time slots when this may occur are before 8:00 am, during the lunch hour, and after 5:00 pm. During these times, the gatekeeper might not be in the office or at their desk and target prospects might answer their own calls.

Dealing with Automated Attendant

Unfortunately, dealing with the automated attendants can sometimes be just as or more difficult than dealing with the live gatekeepers. The main tactic to try when you have to go through one of these is to try to get to a live person as quickly as possible.

Some systems will direct you to an operator or switchboard if you press "0" or if you say "operator". If that does not work, one tactic to use is to enter a random set of digits to try to get to get to any employee's desk. Of course, the person you reach will likely not be anywhere close to the person that you are trying to reach, but she may be able to point you in the right direction and possibly transfer you over.

Don't Take it Personally

The last tactic, and it is actually more of an internal tactic than something that you say or do, is to always remember to not take anything the gatekeeper says personally. This is worth keeping in mind because it is very easy to take it personally when a gatekeeper is rude or rejects your call attempt. You can feel like he is attacking you and not accepting you for who you are and this can be very frustrating and sometimes tear you down if you don't have the right perspective.

The reality is that the gatekeeper does not know who you are or anything about you. As a result, when he is being difficult, it has nothing to do with you. If anything, it is more about the company that you represent, or that you are just one of the many outsiders that are trying to get in and the gatekeeper is just doing his best to keep all the outsiders out. And when he is being somewhat ugly, keep in mind that his job can often be difficult and unpleasant, and that can feed into the way gatekeepers treat sales people like you.

9

PAIN

IDENTIFYING WHAT IS NOT WORKING

Great Spirit – Grant that I may not criticize my neighbor until I have walked a mile in his moccasins.

LAKOTA SIOUX

One of the most important things that you need to accomplish during a cold call is to uncover pain prospect is experiencing. This step is critical due to the fact that being able to consistently find pain will help you to keep conversations going and improve the potential for creating leads. On the other hand, finding out that the prospect does not have pain will allow you to identify that you might need to move on to find better prospects to spend our valuable time with.

WHAT IS PAIN?

Pain in this context does not mean literal, physical discomfort; rather, it is essentially the negative impact felt by your prospect when something is not working well or could be working better. One very basic way to look at this is to try to figure out if a prospect is great, good, OK, or could be better in the areas that your products impact. If the findings are that things are great or good, there might not be any pain. If things are OK or could be better, there could be something going on that is causing some sort of pain.

WHY PAIN IS IMPORTANT

This is one of the most important concepts to embrace when trying to improve cold calling. Here are a few points as to why:

No Pain – No Reason to Meet

As discussed in Chapter 2, the best goal for a cold call may be to get the prospect to agree to a first conversation. But if you do not uncover any pain that the prospect is experiencing in the area that our products or services pertain to, then there is no real reason for the prospect to meet with you beyond the cold call.

To demonstrate this, let's use an example of a doctor's office placing a cold call to a potential patient. Of course this does not happen in the real world, but below are two extreme scenarios that we can look at to see how important pain is.

Scenario A – No Pain

Caller: *"Hi, this is Dr. White's office. How are you feeling?"*

Prospect: *"I feel great. Never better."*

Caller: *"Oh, I see. Would you like me to schedule an appointment for you next week to run some tests on you?"*

Prospect: *"No, I feel great. No need. Thank you for your call."*

Scenario B – Extreme Pain

Caller: *"Hi, this is Dr. White's office. How are you feeling?"*

Prospect: *"Horrible. My head is pounding. Can't sleep. Can't eat."*

Caller: *"Oh, I see. Would you like me to schedule an appointment for you next week?"*

Prospect: *"Yes. But is next week the earliest I can get in?"*

What we can take from that example is that when your goal is to transition to a first conversation or schedule an appointment, if you don't find any pain, it might not make sense for the prospect to meet with you. And to take that one step further, if we can't find any pain, it also does not make sense to spend your valuable time meeting with the prospect, as you would be spending time with a prospect who does not have a high probability of purchasing anything.

No Pain – No Change

Let's look at a scenario where there was no pain identified, but thanks to your awesome sales skills you were still able to get a meeting with a prospect and create a lead. In this scenario, the prospect may be very excited and interested in your products and services, but when you get to the end of the sales cycle and it is time to get the prospect to execute the transaction and spend money, things could possibly stall out or the purchase could get canceled due to the fact that the prospect does not really need what we have to offer. In simpler terms, if there is no pain there is no reason to change.

Gets the Prospect's Attention

When you are on a cold call, one of the most effective ways to help establish the call and keep it going is to get the prospect's attention and uncovering pain will help tremendously with this. By getting the conversation centered on what the prospect is having trouble with, you will greatly increase your likelihood of grabbing and keeping the prospect's attention. Conversely, if you try to establish a cold call and the topic of discussion is not connected to any area of pain or priority, you are not going to be building a conversation that is interesting and attention grabbing for the prospect.

Builds a Connection with the Prospect

When you are able to focus a discussion around a prospect's pain, you are more likely to build a better connection and rapport with that prospect. This is a result of a few different factors. First, you will be talking about something that is important to him versus wasting his time talking about something that is important to you. You will also be giving off a fairly polished image of yourself by being sophisticated enough to understand what is going on with the prospect and to know that is an important area to discuss. And lastly, a pain focused conversation is more of a "all about you" conversation versus an "all about me" conversation. When you add all of this up, you may find the prospect respecting and appreciating you more and this can foster a stronger connection.

Valuable Information

If you are able to find out what is not working well or could be working better for a prospect, you will have just uncovered extremely valuable information. This is information that can be used during every step of the sales cycle. You can use this to schedule a first appointment and then to build your business case and any ROI (return on investment) calculations. And if you find yourself where the deal is stalling out at the end of the sales cycle when you are trying to close, you can always circle back to the pain that the prospect is having.

Qualify Better

If you are not able to identify any pain that the prospect has, that means that everything is going well for the prospect. If things are going well, there will not be a significant amount of motivation for the prospect to make a change. If there is not motivation to make a change, even if the prospect shows a level of interest, he might not be qualified. Even if the prospect is available to attend demos and meetings, when it comes time for him to pull the trigger in terms of making a commitment or spending money, the deal may stall or get killed because there might not be enough motivation. As a result, uncovering pain is a key step to qualifying the prospect.

THREE LEVELS OF PAIN

In Chapter 3, we discussed three levels of value that you offer – Technical, Business, and Personal. We can use that same structure of levels when we try to think about the different areas that prospects may have pain.

Technical Pain

If something is not working well, there is likely pain being felt at a technical level. This would be the impact that is at the lowest level and is as close to the problem as possible. Technical pain can usually be felt close to the processes, systems, and people that support the business and operation.

For example, if a company's website goes down, this means that customers are not able to access the site and orders are not able to be processed. The technical pain that results from this is that processes will fail and stop working, transactions will not be able to be processed, technical staff will need to be dispatched to try to resolve the problem, and new hardware or software may need to be installed to fix the problem and prevent it from occurring again.

Business Pain

When technical pain is created, this will typically work its way up and create some sort of pain or impact at the business level. This is typically the pain that is felt or seen in areas like revenue, costs, and services.

If you continue with the same scenario of a website going down, all of the technical pain that the company experiences will float up to the business level in the form of poor delivery of services leading to missed sales and lost revenue. There would also likely be business pain in the form of increased costs resulting from the resources that the company needs to pay to resolve the problem, plus the cost for the equipment that needs to be fixed or upgraded to ensure the outage does not happen again. In the longer term, there could be some business pain felt in terms of lost market share due to the loss of existing customers and future prospects.

Personal Pain

One area of pain that can often get overlooked is the component of personal pain. This is the pain that floats up to have negative impacts on a prospect's personal interests like income, career, and work environment. While we all work hard at our jobs and our work may contribute to a larger cause, at the end of the day, we all have a self-serving part of us that makes us concerned with things like compensation, job security, career growth, workload, recognition, politics, work-life balance, our families, etc. When something is not working well, the pain can easily have a ripple effect and reach the prospect in these personal areas.

If we are an employee for a company where the website goes down, this could cause us personal pain, as we could end up working long hours if we are part of the team that needs to resolve the problem. This pain can be felt in the form of a heavy workload of hours, which can lead to discomfort and take away time that could be spent with our family. If we are a senior manager and this happens on our watch, problems like this could impact our job security and decrease the potential for a promotion. All of the situations just described cause personal pain because they directly impact us at a personal level.

SIX PAIN SYMPTOMS

If being a sales person is similar to being a doctor, where you need to be able to figure out if there is pain and where it is, then you need to be able to know what to look for in terms of symptoms. To improve your ability to identify pain symptoms, you can use six different categories of symptoms as a guide to know what to look for.

To help outline these six categories and identify how they differ from one another, we will use an example that just about everybody can relate to: owning and operating a vehicle. In this scenario, imagine that we use this vehicle to perform work-related activities, and the primary activity is to complete deliveries.

1. Not working well

If we own a vehicle and it happens to have mechanical challenges and breaks down from time-to-time, this will likely cause a pain symptom of things not working well.

Symptom: The vehicle breaks down or does not start three or four times a year.

Root cause: The systems and processes internal to the vehicle are old or faulty and not working well.

Technical pain: We will not be able to get to our destination when the problem occurs.

Business pain: We are not able to complete deliveries, and this causes a decrease in revenue and customer satisfaction.

Personal pain: We have to work late when this occurs, and that takes away time we would normally spend with our family.

Just about every business has some form of the symptom of things not working well. Common examples of this are businesses that use old or outdated technology. Similar to an old car that breaks down, these systems often fail, and this can cause pain at all three levels.

2. Could be working better

Let's change the scenario by saying we have a vehicle that is very reliable and never breaks, but there is room for improvement in the way that it performs. For example, while the vehicle starts like a charm, its level of acceleration and top speed are less than the average vehicle on the road.

Symptom: The vehicle is not able to travel as fast as we would like or need.

Root cause: We are not using the right size or type of vehicle for our needs.

Technical pain: It takes us a little longer than needed to get to each destination, and this decreases the number of deliveries that we can complete.

Business pain: By us not being able to complete as many deliveries as we could with a faster vehicle, we are missing out on potential revenue, and this creates an opportunity cost.

Personal pain: Since we are not able to complete as many deliveries, our monthly bonuses will be less and this has a negative impact on our compensation.

This pain can be seen in the business world where a business has adequate and reliable systems and processes that get the job done, but the systems and infrastructure are not as productive or as scalable as needed. For example, take a manufacturing line that produces 100 units per hour. If there are better systems that could be used that would lead to 250 units per hour, this could be causing a pain symptom of things could be working better.

3. Time consuming

Let's adjust the scenario so that our vehicle is both reliable and performs at the level that we need it to, but in this case the vehicle has very manual controls and features. Features like transmission, windows, locks, entertainment, climate, and lights must be manually controlled and adjusted.

Symptom: It is time consuming to perform all the routine tasks needed to operate the vehicle.

Root cause: We have very manual processes and systems in our vehicle.

Technical pain: It can be very time consuming and labor intensive to fully operate the vehicle. This could result in it taking more time to get to each destination because our operation of the vehicle is slowed.

Business pain: Since our vehicle is manual and this negatively impacts our speed and efficiency, we cannot complete as many deliveries in a day and this negatively impacts our revenue.

Personal impact: Since we are not able to complete as many deliveries, our monthly bonuses will be less and this has a negative impact on our compensation.

This symptom is common in the business world where a business has very manual and time consuming processes and this causes pain at all three levels. Through either process improvements or through the use of technology and automation, many processes can be made more efficient, saving time, decreasing pain, decreasing costs, and increasing revenue.

4. Potential for errors

We have identified a problem with our vehicle in which our speedometer sporadically displays the incorrect rate of speed that we are traveling.

Symptom: Our speedometer displays the incorrect speed.

Root cause: The speedometer is flawed and not working correctly.

Technical pain: We never know how fast we are going, and this can impair our ability to properly operate the vehicle.

Business pain: These errors could increase the potential for us to exceed the speed limit, and that could result in traffic violations and accidents.

Personal pain: Operating the vehicle with unreliable information could make it unsafe, and this could potentially lead to physical injury.

This is a very common pain symptom in the business world, as both people and automated systems sometimes make errors. Errors can have a severe impact on a business and can not only result in increased cost or lost revenue, but can also lead to legal implications with fines and lawsuits. At a personal level, errors could impact the health and safety of the employees.

5. High costs

Another very common scenario is that our vehicle is not fuel efficient, which results in high costs.

Symptom: We have high fuel expenses.

Root cause: Our vehicle is not fuel efficient. This could be a result of the type of vehicle that we are driving, but could also be a result of the performance or health of the vehicle, as there could be a fuel leak or the system might not be operating perfectly.

Technical pain: This lack of fuel efficiency means we must stop to refill our fuel more than we would like to, and this is costing us valuable time.

Business impact: We are spending more money and time on fuel, and this is impacting both revenue and profitability.

Personal impact: The high costs are impacting profitability, and that will decrease our profit sharing cut at the end of the year.

Just about every business has room for improvement in the area of high costs or a need to decrease costs. The key here is to identify the root cause of high costs and the impact associated with those. If we are selling a solution that can eliminate or mitigate the root cause and decrease costs, we could find ourselves in a very productive discussion.

6. Low revenue

We use the vehicle for deliveries and we are not making as much money as we would like.

Symptom: We have lower revenue than we would like.

Root cause: There could be many root causes for this symptom, but if we are looking solely at the vehicle, this could be a byproduct of some of the challenges already discussed, which are that the vehicle is either not reliable, performing well, or efficient, and that is decreasing our ability to optimize the use of the vehicle.

Technical pain: By not getting the most out of the vehicle, we are not able to complete as many deliveries in a day as we could with a better vehicle.

Business pain: By not accomplishing as many deliveries as we could with a better vehicle, our overall revenue is lower than it could be.

Personal pain: The low revenue is impacting profitability, and that will decrease our profit sharing cut at the end of the year.

Regardless of industry or profit versus nonprofit, every business has a desire to increase revenue. And if you flip that around, that means they all should have a pain symptom of revenue not being at the level that they would prefer. The key here is to identify the root cause, map the impact, and then try to find out how or if we can help.

CHALLENGES WITH UNCOVERING PAIN

Now that we have outlined what pain is and how valuable it can be to the cold calling process, it is time for some bad news: Uncovering pain while on a cold call can be fairly difficult. This is a result of two very consistent factors.

State of Denial

The first factor is that a prospect who has answered a cold call might not be eager to open up and share information in terms of what he wants or what he needs to improve, especially if he has a high level of interest in ending the call. Even if you ask the prospect a question that directly strikes a chord, he may not acknowledge that he has pain in that area.

It's kind of like a football coach asking a player that just took a hard hit how he feels. The player may have pain but his primary desire is to get back in the game, so if he is asked about pain, his quick answer may often be "I'm fine," and the pain is denied. If someone wants to get off of a cold call and get back to work (back in the game), he may just dismiss or not acknowledge pain in the same way.

Latent Pain

The second reason that uncovering pain can be challenging is that many of the prospects might not be fully aware of the pain that they have. When the prospect has pain but is not aware of it, he has what is called latent pain. The pain exists but the prospect is either completely unaware of it or it is just not at the forefront of his mind.

Let's go back to the six pain symptoms that we went through and the vehicle example. If you look at the all of the different pain symptoms and associated problems, it could realistically be the case that any of those problems discussed, aside from the vehicle physically breaking down, could be occurring without the driver being aware that the problem exists. In other words, the driver could be using the vehicle and either thinking it is operating properly, or as well as needed, and be oblivious to the pain and impact that is outlined in each of those scenarios – errors are occurring, things are time consuming, costs are high, things could be better, revenue is low. If that is the case, the driver has pain, but it is latent pain.

FOUR TACTICS TO UNCOVER PAIN

While pain can be challenging to find on a cold call, it is not impossible. Here are four tactics that are fairly simple and easy to implement that can increase your ability to get pain to the forefront of conversations while cold calling.

1. Ask rating questions

One tactic to use to uncover pain is to ask rating questions. Rating questions ask the prospect to answer a question by answering on a scale from one to ten. For example, "How happy are you with the level of service from your current provider, on a scale from one to ten?" This is a much more powerful question than just, "How happy are you with the level of service from your current provider?"

One benefit from this type of question is that it gives you a little more information as the answer is a little more detailed and precise. Continuing with the example above, without the rating part of the question, the prospect may have said, "We are very happy." But if you ask him to rate his happiness, he may give you a score of eight. This helps you to gather more detailed answers, which is good, but the real power is what you can do after we get the rating

Regardless of the rating that the prospect gives, you then have the opportunity to politely inquire as to why he answered with his rating and this can help to uncover pain. Continuing again with the same example, the prospect said he was very happy and gave a rating of eight. But why does he feel it is an eight and not a ten? Obviously, there is some sort of gap there and you can politely ask, "Oh, great. Do you mind if I ask why you answered with a rating of eight rather than a ten?" "What could be changed to get you to improve your rating from an eight to a ten?" The answers here may help you to uncover something that is not working well.

2. Provide pain examples

Another tactic to use to uncover pain is to share examples of pain that other prospects or clients of yours have experienced. Then follow that by asking if the prospect can relate to any of the examples or if he has experienced anything similar. If there is an acknowledgement from the prospect that he can relate to any of the examples, you have just uncovered pain, and you can then drill deeper by asking questions to get the prospect to share more details.

To provide an example of this, let's assume that we sell accounting software that has a global reporting feature which is better than the competition's. In order to find qualified prospects that would benefit from this feature, we want to find prospects who are having challenges running a global report. To help us find out if the prospects have pain in that area, we can provide an example of pain by saying, "We work with a lot with businesses that say it is time consuming and difficult to run a global report. Is that something that you can relate to?"

From there, the prospect will then either share similar pain, will share pain in a different area, or will let us know that they do not have any pain. We can drill down into any pain that is uncovered and if there is not any, we can try to share another pain example. If the prospect does not connect with a couple of different pain examples, we can simply move on to another question or discussion thread.

3. Ask wish list questions

Wish list questions can sometimes uncover pain. These basically get the prospect to explore things they would wish to have or wish to have changed if they could have their way. Below are some examples of wish list questions:

> "If you could wave a wand and have any functionality added to your current system, what would you add?"
>
> "If you could eliminate any of the existing challenges, which would you get rid of first?"
>
> "If you could eliminate any of the existing manual processes, which would you automate first?"

It is important to listen closely to the answers as they can likely be tied back to some sort of pain. The answer will not always sound like pain, but if you drill into why the prospect is wishing for whatever he listed out, you can likely tie it to some sort of pain symptoms. To help with this, explore why he provided the answer he did and try to identify how he is currently being impacted by not having what he would wish for. If there is some sort of noticeable and negative impact by not having what he wants or needs, you might be very close to uncovering some pain.

4. Disqualify the prospect

When you have tried everything and you cannot get the prospect to share or admit to any pain, you can try to disqualify the prospect as your last resort tactic. We outlined the concept of disqualifying in Chapter 7 and the way to apply this to trying to find pain is to say something like, "Well, it sounds like you all are doing pretty good."

When you say that, you are likely going to get one of two responses. Either the prospect will agree with you and confirm the disqualification or the prospect will challenge your disqualification attempt and tell you where things are not great. This may trigger something and if not, you can begin to label the prospect as not having any pain and begin to move on.

MAPPING PAIN IMPACT

If you are able to uncover pain the prospect is experiencing, you can then take that one step further by trying to determine the impact of the pain. Mapping out how the pain is impacting the prospect at a technical, business, and personal level will provide valuable information.

We basically demonstrated identifying impact when we went through each of the pain symptom examples. We started with a problem and identified how that is impacting the driver of the vehicle on a technical, business and personal level.

You can do that same progression when talking with a prospect when you identify something that is not working well or could be working better. You can inquire as to how a particular problem or challenge is impacting processes, systems, or people (technical impact). After you gather some details in that area, you can try to learn more about the impact on revenue, costs, or services (business impact). And if appropriate, you may inquire as to how the prospect is being impacted in terms of career, income, or work environment (personal impact).

Magnifying Pain

As you discuss the impact the pain is causing, you will stand to either magnify or minimize the pain. Magnifying the pain occurs when you identify that the impact is noticeable or significant. Being able to magnify pain will help build deal momentum.

To go through a quick example of this, we will use a scenario of a doctor talking to a patient where knee pain has been uncovered. Once the pain is discovered, the doctor asks the patient how the knee pain is impacting her and learns that the pain has prevented the patient from running every morning and this is causing major disruptions in the patient's life in terms of physical and mental health. These changes are having a ripple effect to impact the patient on both a professional and personal level in terms of relationships. By mapping out the impact of the pain, the doctor not only learned a tremendous amount about what the patient is experiencing, but also magnified the pain from what was originally discovered.

What we can take from this example is that once the doctor and patient become aware of the large impact, they can reach a decision where it makes sense to take action and make a change. If investment of time and money in the form of surgery and physical rehabilitation is the solution to eliminating the pain, the patient will be more able to justify the investment by being fully aware of the current impact of the pain.

The same relationship can exist with a prospect when we are able to magnify their pain. If continuing through your sales process will require time and an investment of money from the prospect, by helping to make the prospect aware of the impact of staying the course with the existing pain, you will be better able to motivate and justify continued forward movement.

Minimizing Pain

But let's look at the other extreme of that example before we move on. Going back to the medical example, let's say that the doctor asks about the impact of the pain and learns that it is no big deal really. The patient is still able to do everything that she wants to and is not too bothered. In this scenario, instead of magnifying pain, the doctor actually minimized the pain and identified that there is not really much of an overall impact. This is very valuable information as the doctor just identified that there is no need and justification for any treatment.

Applying this to working with a prospect, you could find yourself in a scenario where you uncover pain but when you map the impact, you uncover that there is minimal to no impact. When this is the case, the prospect may not be motivated and able to justify spending time and money to decrease the pain due to the lack of any real negative impacts. While this discovery is not something to get excited over, it is an important thing to identify as it can tell you when to walk away and move on try to find prospects that have greater needs and that will be more motivated to implement action and change.

10

INTEREST

CREATING MOMENTUM

The virtues and vices are all put in motion by interest.

FRANÇOIS DE LA ROCHEFOUCAULD

Once you have uncovered pain that the prospect is experiencing during a cold call, you can begin to shift toward building interest. This is the point where you begin to discuss how you can help in more detail and why it would make sense for the prospect to spend some of her valuable time talking with you.

To use a sporting analogy, if you were fishing, the point at which you get the prospect talking about pain is where the fish has its mouth around the hook. But before you begin to try to reel in the fish, you want to try to get the fish to bite down on the hook. If you do not, you could begin to reel in before you really have anything on the hook, and this could lead to reeling in an empty hook. The same principle applies with prospects as you need to get them to bite down on the hook by creating interest, before you try to reel them in.

TACTICS TO BUILD INTEREST

It may be easy to think that you do not have a lot of control or influence over the level of interests that builds on the prospect's side. And that she will either like and need the product that you sell or she won't. The reality is that you do have a tremendous amount of influence over your prospect's interest and there are very clear and practical things you can do to trigger it. Here are seven tactics that you can use.

1. Connect Pain to Value

At this point, you have begun to get your hands around the value that you offer. You have also begun to think more about the prospect pain that you help to resolve. When you have some details identified in those two areas, you can combine some of those valuable points to produce some value statements that connect prospect pain with the value that you have to offer.

Here is an example of a statement that connects pain with technical and business value:

> "We help businesses to deal with not having enough leads (pain) and do this by improving the training for the frontline sales resources (technical value) and this can typically lead to improved lead generation and lower sales staff turnover (business value)."

2. Communicate How You Differ

One powerful way to build interest is to communicate to prospects how you differ from your competitors. This could either be a statement that either highlights your strengths or you could come at this from the other side and highlight your competitor's weaknesses.

Here is an example of a statement that highlights three areas of differentiation:

"Some ways that we differ from other options out there are that our CRM and email marketing are combined in one system, we offer the industries best service and support, and our software is designed by sales people for sales people."

3. Communicate Historical ROI Data

We have discussed improving your ability to communicate the value that you have to offer. That can help you to grab a prospect's attention and improve your ability to effectively communicate what you have to offer. But to build interest, you need to take that one step further and begin talk about how that value translates to dollars and return on investment.

The main thing that your prospect cares about is "what is in it for me". And while talking about your value begins to answer that, it is the ROI that the prospect can expect to see and the amount of time it takes for him to get his money back that really starts to build interest.

To give you some material to use here, look across your customer base and try to gather some data on how you have helped your customers from a quantitative standpoint. That can help you to develop some statements that you can share with prospects, and you can either provide some exact examples with real numbers or you can be a little less specific and just share some ranges. Here are some examples:

"We worked with Fuel Strike and helped them to decrease their labor costs by 20% by helping to decrease absenteeism."

"Most of our clients see a 15% to 20% decrease in labor costs by using our systems to decrease absenteeism and that can typically lead to a payback point on their investment in 12 to 18 months."

4. Threats from Doing Nothing

One very powerful way to build interest is to educate your prospects on what could happen if they do not purchase from you or any of your competitors. You basically want to paint the picture of what could happen or continue to happen if the prospect does not purchase something. This is a more effective tactic when you are competing against the status quo versus competing against another vendor.

A prime example of this is when a sales person selling flood insurance talks to a prospect about what could happen if there is a severe storm and focuses on the details around potential damages and costs for repairs. The potential outcome of having to spend $50K to $100K on house repairs if there is a flood is an example of a threat from doing nothing when choosing to not purchase flood insurance.

When a prospect that is leaning toward the status quo pictures the possibilities and threats, her level of interest can increase. Here is an example of what that might look like:

"Some things you might want to think about with not doing anything in this area are that a storm can happen without warning and easily cause between $50,000 to $100,000 in damages and you could have to pay out of pocket for those repairs if you do not have any coverage in this area."

For an example with a little less of obvious of a threat, let's take a sales person that sells software that helps to automate manual processes. To help paint a picture of the threat of doing nothing to a prospect that is leaning toward the status quo, she can discuss the costs from lost productivity by continuing to use the existing manual processes. Here is an example of that:

"Our software would be around $100,000. But if you continue with your manual processes, your annual cost per year with the additional labor that you currently use is $300,000. In addition, your probability for errors will by higher and that could lead to higher product returns and lost customers, both negatively hitting the bottom line."

5. Paint a Future State Picture

One very effective way to create interest on a cold call is to try to paint a picture for the prospect for where he could be if he purchased from you.

This can be accomplished in a couple of quick statements, but to get there, simply describe the potential future state an ideal client would reach from realizing the value that your products and services have to offer. From there, try to describe this in a way so that he can picture it being achievable and happening to him.

For example, if you sold some sort of training or educational product, you could describe to the prospect the level of mastery and success they could reach by going through your program. You could say something like:

> "If you read this book and apply the concepts in it, you can drastically improve your cold calling skills and results. This can lead to a tremendous improvement in your sales performance in the short-term. In the long-term your improved performance can lead to significant career and financial growth. This transformation will not only have a positive impact on you; it could have a ripple affect that impacts your entire family."

6. Tell a Client Story

Another way that you can communicate what you have to offer and build interest is to share a story about another client you have worked with. If you can share a story of another company that had similar challenges and explain how you helped to drive positive improvements and share where the company ended up in terms of results, you can make large strides in terms of building interest.

The more parallels that you can establish between your story and the prospect you are talking to, the more powerful your story will be. In addition, if you know where the prospect would like to go in terms of a desired state and you can tell a story that demonstrates how you helped another company to get there, you are likely to grab her attention and build interest.

7. Company Facts

The last tactic that we will outline is one that we believe to be the least powerful, and ironically it is one that sales people some time lead with, and that is to share some of the company facts and bragging points. Here is an example:

"Some other details about us is that we have been in business for 30 years, have won the Pioneer Award for customer service for 5 out of the past 6 years, and we do not outsource any of our development."

These are good points to share with prospects but we recommend sharing these toward the end of your attempt to build interest. Where some sales people go wrong is they share these details at the beginning of a cold call before they have done any of the fundamental steps like communicating value, qualifying, and finding pain. When that is done, you might reach a point where a prospect hears the company facts and thinks "So what?". But if you go through the key steps and then use some of the other more powerful building interest tactics, there is definitely a place after that for sharing some of the company facts and bragging points.

DELIVER SILVER BULLETS

We just gave you a number of things to add to your arsenal. But unfortunately, when applying this to cold calling, you still have to operate with the mindset that time and attention are limited and you need to be as efficient as possible. That being the case, one thing that you can do is develop a list of powerful silver bullet points. These are one sentence statements that utilize any of the seven tactics previously discussed. Once you we have this list, you can share a few points on a cold call to try to trigger interest. Here are some examples of some short, yet powerful, silver bullet points:

- We helped many companies in the manufacturing industry to decrease the cost of goods sold by between 10 to 15 percent
- Investments in our products typically reach a payback in 18 months
- One way that we differ from other options out there is that our system only uses one database
- Our products are easy to get up and running and use and can be implemented without the need for any consulting services

An important detail on using silver bullets is to not read through them like a list of features on a brochure. Have the list in front of you and pick a couple that you feel might resonate well with the prospect based on what she has shared so far. If the conversation up until that point has not provided enough information to enable you to know what points fit best, just share a few that you think will get the most attention.

An ideal time to deliver some building interest silver bullets on a cold call is after you have performed some qualifying and maybe uncovered some pain. At that point, you may have the prospect's attention (the hook is in the mouth) and you just want to get a little more interest (get the prospect to bite down) before you go for the close for a first conversation.

11

RAPPORT

BUILDING STRONG
CONNECTIONS

Better than a thousand hollow words,
is one word that brings peace.

BUDDHA

In order to be a consistent and effective sales professional, it is critical to be effective at building rapport with prospects and customers. Executing well in this area is important not only because people buy from people they like, but, more importantly, because having rapport will greatly improve a sales person's ability to control and manage an opportunity throughout the sales cycle. Applying that to cold calling, you will be more likely to keep the cold call going and transition to a first conversation when you are able to create some level of rapport with the prospect.

RAPPORT-BUILDING TACTICS

It may be common to believe that your ability to build rapport with the prospect is purely based on the prospect liking your personality. And if that is the main factor—and if you kind of are who you are at this point in your life—you could fall into believing that rapport is either going to naturally build or it is not, and there is not much that you can do to positively impact that. But the reality is that you do have control over rapport, as there are some very clear and easy-to-implement things that you can do to build and trigger stronger connections with others.

Display Humility

One thing that you can do to create a better connection with prospects is to display humility. This is a little counterintuitive, as we have always been taught to act confident and assertive when dealing with prospects. Displaying humility is somewhat the opposite of that: it would mean presenting yourself as more modest, human, and capable of making mistakes or not knowing everything.

Of course, when working in sales, you want to be confident in who you are, in the products you sell, and in the company you work for. But to show the prospect at different times that you are human and in some ways very normal or average can help to create a more friendly and personal relationship.

An example of this is admitting to the prospect that you don't know the answer to a question being asked or taking ownership of a mistake. These two scenarios are examples in which an ultra-aggressive sales person might try to avoid any negative light being shined on him. But to step up and show the confidence to take ownership of a mistake or lack of knowledge will display humility, and this will show that you are human, down to earth, and relatable, and could possibly have a positive impact on rapport.

Of course, what you do right after you display moments of humility will be important in maintaining credibility. For example, it is powerful to admit that you do not know the answer to the question. But it is critical to follow that up by communicating how and when the answer will be found and then successfully delivering on that promise.

Compliment the Competition

Another counterintuitive tactic is to give a compliment to the competition. An example of this is sharing something that your competition does well, if you know that the prospect is currently doing business or is considering doing business with the competitor. Of course, you will want to follow this up with some areas in which the competition might have weaknesses or where you clearly have strengths over them.

By sharing something positive about the competition, you will accomplish some very clear and powerful things in that exact moment. First, you will show a tremendous amount of confidence in yourself and your products if you are not afraid to share something good about the competition. Secondly, you will present yourself as more of an advisor than a sales person, as you will be sharing valuable and what appears to be unbiased information. And when you share what is good about the competition, you will also stand to improve your level of believability regarding what you share about your company and products as we will appear more honest and trustworthy.

Disqualify the Prospect

Sticking with the theme of counterintuitive tactics, you can also increase rapport by disqualifying the prospect. We have already discussed the concept of disqualifying in detail in Chapter 7. By disqualifying, you are likely to instantly decrease the prospect's guard, as he may view you as looking out for his best interest. By making the prospect feel like you are putting his interest before your primary interest of closing sales, you are likely to positively impact the level of rapport.

Understand the Prospect

We as humans have an internal need to be understood. When you are able to make a prospect feel like you understand her in terms of her challenges, what her goals are, and what she is trying to say, you will take huge strides toward building rapport. Some of the next tactics will help you to sub-communicate to prospects that you understand them.

Respect the Prospect's Time

A very minor tactic that you can implement to positively impact rapport is to always respect the prospect's time. If you are calling her, you need to make sure she is available and you are not interrupting anything. One way to effectively do this is to always ask at the beginning of a cold call if you are catching the prospect in the middle of anything. This subtle question will show that you respect the prospect's time and can spike the level of rapport that you have with the prospect.

If you are attending a scheduled meeting with her, you need to confirm that she is still available and confirm if there is a particular time when she needs the meeting to end. You can take that one step further by demonstrating during the meeting that you are aware of the time and managing the flow of the meeting so that you do not overextend what the prospect has given you.

When a prospect sees that you respect her time, this will potentially increase rapport in two ways. First, by you respecting her time, you are clearly demonstrating that you have respect for her. When you show respect for her, she may begin to have respect for you. In addition, by you showing that you respect her time, you will sub-communicate that you understand her and what it is like working with her busy and hectic schedule. These minor increases in mutual respect and understanding can have a direct impact on the level of rapport.

Focus on the Prospect's Interests

As humans, we are all self-absorbed to a certain degree. So we gain more enjoyment when conversations revolve around topics that we have interest in or are knowledgeable about. To play into that dynamic, if you keep discussions with prospects in areas that they either have interest or are knowledgeable about, you can stand to create more interesting conversations for the prospect. If prospects find the conversations they have with you to be interesting, you can stand to see an improvement in rapport.

Areas where you can be pretty safe to assume the prospect has interest and knowledge are her business, her company, and her job. If you consciously try to keep conversations focused in those areas, you can improve your ability to keep her attention and build interest. This may sound like common sense, but it can be easy for us to do the exact opposite of this on cold calls, as we can easily direct the conversation to our interests by talking about our products and our company. If you hold off on this urge and shift the conversation away from you and shift to make sure it is focused on the prospect, you can stand to create a more interesting and engaging conversation and this can help to build rapport.

Listen to the Prospect

In addition to getting the conversation focused on topics that the prospect is interested in, you can continue to increase rapport by demonstrating that you are closely listening to what the prospect says. By simply listening, you can give off some powerful sub-communications:

Respect for what they say: If you listen intently, you will show that you have respect for what your prospects are thinking and saying.

Displays you understand them: If you show prospects that you are listening, you will stand to make them feel like you understand them.

Increase their respect for you: If you demonstrate a strong ability to listen and are taking notes while prospects are speaking, this will give the impression that you are competent, and this could increase their level of respect for you.

Allows them do more of the talking: If you can shift from talking to listening, prospects will be talking more. This can make the prospects more engaged in you and in your conversation, as not only will they be investing more into the conversation by talking, but also because many prospects will enjoy having the spotlight shined more on them.

Here are a few very clear and easy ways to sub-communicate that you are listening to prospects:

Eye contact: At the simplest level, maintaining eye contact is a clear way to show that you are listening. (Not applicable when cold calling)

Nonverbal confirmation: In addition to eye contact, you can use nonverbal cues like nodding your head to signal back to the prospect that you are hearing what she is saying. (Not applicable while cold calling)

Verbal confirmation: When you are on the phone, you cannot perform a head nod but you can deliver the same signal with verbal phrases like "I see," "OK," "I understand," etc.

Reframing: A very powerful way to show a prospect that you are listening to her is to take what she has shared and share it back to her in a summary that is in your own words. This will not only show that you are listening, but will also show that you understand what she saying.

Taking notes: Another nonverbal cue that you are listening is to physically take notes in front of the prospect as she talks. (Not applicable while cold calling)

Move Forward on the Prospect's Terms

It is understandable to believe that you must always push the prospect to move to the next step and that you must get her to move forward as quickly as possible. With a need to close deals always at the forefront of our mind and with the fact that prospects are not likely to chase us, we simply have a natural mindset to try to push things along. The one challenge with that is that if you are too pushy, you can negatively impact the level of rapport that you have with the prospect. And if being too pushy can decrease rapport, it makes sense to assume that if you do the opposite of being pushy with the prospect, you could stand to increase rapport.

Being too pushy could be accomplished by calling a prospect too much and trying to get her to meet or move forward before she is ready. One simple way to decrease or avoid that level of pushiness is to simply call and meet with the prospect at a pace that she is comfortable with. To achieve this, you can move forward on the prospect's terms by letting her advise as to what direction to go and when.

Here are some questions that demonstrate letting the prospect lead. Note how these questions differ from the typical language from a pushy sales person. This is the type of language that builds rapport and relationships.

"What direction do you want to go?"

"What do you want to do next?"

"When would you like me to check back with you?"

"When would you like to meet again?"

It is important to note that this approach is only good if you have executed well in other key areas, like qualifying the prospect, identifying pain, building interest, trial closing, building pipeline, etc. If you have checked those boxes, you can have more confidence in letting the prospect lead. But if you have not executed well in most of those areas and you then let the prospect lead, she may lead you to nowhere. For example, if you have not qualified, triggered any interest, or built any rapport, the timing that the prospect would want to talk again might possibly be never.

12

CREDIBILITY

INSTILLING CONFIDENCE

It isn't what you do, but how you do it.

JOHN WOODEN

There are two different times during cold calling when it is helpful to establish some sort of credibility. First, when you face gatekeepers who are trying to screen you out, establishing credibility can sometimes help them to decrease their level of guardedness and feel more comfortable letting you in. The second scenario where you can benefit from credibility is when you are dealing with target prospects and need to either get their attention or get their commitment to continue.

One of the reasons that credibility is important is that we face fierce competition every day. We are either competing with a number of other businesses and sales people or we are competing against the prospect's option to do nothing and the status quo. If you don't establish credibility, you may just blend in with the rest of the pesky cold callers and may get denied by the "sales filter." That being the case, there are some very clear and simple things you can do to increase your level of credibility.

ESTABLISH SOCIAL PROOF

When gatekeepers and target prospects answer the phone and recognize that they do not know who you are and why you are calling, their level of guard will immediately go to a medium level. From that point on, everything that you say and do will either make their guard go up or down. The more effective you are at getting prospects to lower their guard, the more successful you will be. And using a tactic of social proof is one way to do that.

Social proof is a concept in which someone is able to establish credibility and a higher level of value and power by connecting himself with certain members of a social group or organization. For example, a host of a party will know just about everybody at the party and as a result of having those connections and existing relationships, he will have extremely high social proof. On the other extreme, a guest at the same party who only knows the host will be more of an outsider and have very low social proof.

Through their actions and communications, both the host and the guest will be sub-communicating to everybody at the party their level of social proof – the host will be talking to just about everybody and the guest may only be talking to one person. If we watched how other guests responded to these two individuals, we may observe that there was less comfort interacting with the guest that was more of an outsider. One factor that this could be traced to is the low social proof and credibility displayed by that guest.

One of the interesting things about social proof is that you have a tremendous amount of control over the level of social proof that you are displaying. Continuing with the example of a guest at a party, if that individual modifies his actions and communications, he can easily increase his level of social proof. For example, by shifting to interact with many different guests of the party, he will give off the image that he has more connections and relationships, and this will immediately sub-communicate a higher level of social proof.

Let's apply this concept to cold calling. When a gatekeeper or target prospect answers your call, he will be immediately trying to determine if you are a friend or a foe. A friend would be someone that he knows in some way or someone who is already on the inside and involved with his company. A foe would be someone on the outside trying to get in, like one of those pesky cold callers. If you can establish social proof, you can stand to get the gatekeeper or prospect to feel like you are more of a friend than a foe, and this will help to decrease his level of guardedness, which could get him to open up more or let you in.

Name Drop Internal Contacts

One effective way to display social proof is to name drop other individuals in the organization whom you have already spoken to or have met with. If you have not had the opportunity to talk to or meet with anybody on the prospect's side, which can likely be the case when cold calling, you can simply name drop individuals you are planning to call or meet with. Here are two examples:

"We have spoken with Maria Gonzales and have collected information on your compliance initiative."

"We are planning on meeting with Maria Gonzales to discuss your compliance initiative."

This tactic can not only improve your credibility and decrease a prospect's guardedness, but it can also improve the prospect's motivation to work with you. Consider if you reach a target prospect and diplomatically name drop his manager or someone above him in the organization and say that you are planning on calling or meeting with the name drop in the near future. There is a very good chance that the person you are talking to will become much more motivated to talk and help you, as the last thing he would want to do is be rude to someone who is going to be talking to other individuals in his organization.

Name Drop Titles

Another tactic to use to create social proof is to name drop titles of the individuals that you work with. If you are trying to sell to a CFO and you mention working with other C-level executives during your cold call, then you sub-communicate that you have experience selling at that level. This minor tactic could have a positive impact on your credibility, as executives prefer to deal with experienced and senior-level sales people.

Name Drop External Contacts and Clients

You can also name drop external contacts and clients to create social proof. Some businesses and communities are fairly small, and people often know their counterparts at other companies. Name dropping a prospect's peer at another company can be a huge help to getting a prospect's attention and can create social proof.

The more common way to use this is to just name drop the client by mentioning the organization as a whole. If you can add a few details around how you have worked with the company and can quantify how you have helped them, you can tremendously improve your position in the conversation.

STORYTELLING

The tactic of storytelling takes social proof and name dropping one step further. You can talk about your features and benefits all day, but what can really paint a picture and establish credibility is telling a story that goes into detail on how you have helped a similar organization.

LACK OF AVAILABILITY

One minor tactic that you can use to try to establish credibility is to display a lack of availability from either a scheduling or product availability standpoint. An example of this is when you discuss either a call back or scheduling a first conversation with a prospect and you display a little difficulty finding a time slot. This can sub-communicate that you are busy, which could mean that you are successful and your products might be good. This is a different message from what is sent when you tell the prospect your calendar is wide open and you can meet at whatever time the prospect is free.

LACK OF NEEDINESS

Similar to the lack of availability tactic is a tactic to display a lack of neediness in terms of needing to close the deal with the prospect. It is not a big secret that sales people want to sell their product, but there is a difference between a sales person who wants to increase sales and do a good job and a sales person who can't sell his products and is struggling to keep his job and possibly pay his bills.

If you are able to display yourself as not needy from a sales standpoint, this can sub-communicate that you are either a good sales person or that you have a quality product, or possibly both, and this can create positive impressions in the area of credibility.

The most effective way to display a lack of neediness is in the way you interact with the prospect when scheduling the next step and how you handle following up. For example, if you let the prospect lead in terms of direction and timing for future discussions by asking, "When would you like to meet again?", you will appear fairly confident and not needy.

And if you stay with that by complying by not following up with him early or trying to push him to move faster than he would prefer, you will continue to maintain a frame of not being needy in terms of closing sales.

If you add to that some disqualifying statements like, "I am not sure if you really need what our services provide" when appropriate, you will add to your image that you are not a needy sales person, and if you add up all of these minor sub-communications, you can see a positive impact in perceived credibility.

CONSENSUS

Similar to the concepts of social proof, lack of availability, and lack of neediness is the concept of creating an image of consensus. Consensus means that a good portion of a group is in agreement about something.

When it comes to your products or services, if we can share information with prospects about our current clients, current orders, lack of product availability, high demand, and full schedule of meetings, this could paint a picture of consensus as there appears to be a large portion of a group in agreement about liking what you have to offer. If there is consensus, this can help to establish credibility.

STATING THE FACTS

As a last resort, you always have the option to simply state the facts of your company and your products to try to establish credibility. For example, you can share the number of years you have been in business, the number of clients that you have, the number of countries that you operate, etc. These are valuable pieces of data and can definitely help to build credibility. But it is important to be aware that the sharing of this type of information is what the average sales person will do to try to create credibility. If you want to stand out from the competition and do it quickly in a cold call setting, you should use more powerful tactics like those shared throughout this chapter.

SECTION III

GAME TIME

13

SCRIPT

KNOW WHAT TO SAY AND ASK

Success depends upon previous preparation, and without such preparation there is sure to be failure.

CONFUCIUS

When you watch the news, stop to think about how well spoken and knowledgeable the news anchor sounds. If you don't think about it, your impression may be that the news person just naturally speaks that way and has a high level of intelligence. But the reality is that the person you are watching has not only written out everything he is saying ahead of time, he has also practiced it over and over, and on top of that, he has his lines in front of him on a teleprompter. We can take a few different lessons from this example of preparation and scripting.

By thoroughly preparing and using a script, the news anchor is able to give off a very strong impression of experience and intelligence. What is interesting here is that in many cases, the news anchor might not be completely an expert on all of the different subjects that he is responsible for reporting on. And the words he is reading are sometimes even written by someone else. Yet, by being prepared and having a guide to read from, he can give off a very strong impression and a much better one than he would if he spoke without a script.

You can apply this same logic to cold calling. By putting together a script for what you are going to say and ask, you can give off a very strong impression and be much more effective. And if you do it the right way, you actually stand to consistently present yourself as experienced and knowledgeable.

One last point on the news anchor example: could you ever imagine a news anchor who had a list of news events and just went on the air and winged it in terms of the wording and flow. He would never do this because the airtime that he has is so precious. You should apply this same logic to cold calling because the time that you get with a prospect, especially if calling at an executive level, is also incredibly precious. If you just try to wing it, you should expect the same low-quality presentation that a news anchor would provide if he just casually talked through the news of the day using the first words that came to his mind.

INCORPORATING A SCRIPT

If you want to sound like the polished news anchor that is on the evening news, it can help to have what you want to say written out in some sort of script ahead of time. Without a script, you are leaning more toward improvising and can create a lot of variability in your results. For example, you may not ask the right questions and deliver the right statements and this can decrease your ability to consistently get the most out of each interaction. If you are not fully capitalizing on the opportunities that you have to interact with prospects, you will not be optimizing your lead generation and sales results.

Even though the benefits of using scripts are strong, many sales people are anti-script and this is usually due to a couple of reasons. First, many sales people think that a script has a negative impact on how you sound when on a call. The argument is that you will sound like you are reading while talking and that will sound amateur and like a telemarketing call. The response to that is, yes, if you do not know your script very well and read directly from it while on a call, you may not make a great impression. But if you use your script properly and use it as a tool to better prepare yourself ahead of time with what you should say and ask while talking with a prospect, and you are familiar enough with the language so that you can use it more as a guide and do not need to read directly from it, you are likely to give off a better impression than you would without a script.

Another reason that scripts aren't often used is that pure laziness comes into play as they can appear to be time consuming to write and memorize. If you are writing a word-for-word script that is long and something that needs to be memorized in full, yes, that can be time consuming and intimidating. One option that is not as cumbersome to incorporate is to use more of a call outline that identifies the key goals, questions, and statements for your call.

THE COLD CALL BLUEPRINT

When an architect designs a house, the process begins with a blueprint. A blueprint provides the structure and outline for the space that will be built, and will be broken down by rooms and each room is clearly designated for a particular purpose. A builder can build 10 homes with the same blueprint and each one will be unique on the inside in terms of decorations. But all will conform to the same flow and design that is provided by the blueprint. You can apply this same concept to your cold call script as you can use a blueprint that breaks the call down into different rooms, or compartments of the call, and that can provide a structure and flow for your script and calls.

Just as a home blueprint will have a room that serves a functional purpose, like a dining room, the cold call blueprint will have compartments and each serve a functional purpose like communicating value, qualifying, finding pain, building interest, closing, etc. And similar to how each home becomes unique with the way it is decorated; each call is unique with the discussion that takes place inside of each compartment. But the blueprint allows you to design the general flow of your ideal call and this can make it easier to learn the scripted points that you develop and better control the different directions that the call can go.

Blueprint Compartments

Here are some compartments that could be part of a cold call blueprint:

Goals of the Call: Just as with anything in life, you have to know where you want a cold call to go in order to increase your chances of successfully getting there. To help with this, your blueprint can outline exactly what you hope to accomplish on each call in terms of both a primary and secondary goal.

Target: The blueprint could include some details around the target area for your prospecting. This could include any valuable details around industry, geography, company size, current state, and title for the prospects that you are trying to reach.

Introduction: Every call you make will have some sort of brief introduction. You can allocate space in your blueprint and script out ahead of time how you decide to introduce yourself in terms of your name and your company and what you initially ask at the very beginning. You may have two different introductions prepared as what you say to a gatekeeper may be different from what you say to a target prospect.

Value Statement: A value statement can be valuable to share early in a cold call. As a result, your cold call blueprint could have a compartment where your value statement is listed out so that you can be reminded to share the value that you offer with the prospects you talk with.

Soft Disqualify Statement: You can deliver a very quick soft disqualify statement early in a call to disarm the prospect and decrease their guard.

Soft Qualifying Questions: In order to make sure that it makes sense for you to spend your valuable time talking with the prospect, you need to ask a few soft qualifying questions during your cold calls and you can have a compartment for where those should fit in your preferred call flow.

Pain Points: It is critical to uncover some sort of pain that the prospect is experiencing in terms of something that is not working well or could be working better during a cold call. If you have a compartment in your cold call blueprint where you focus specifically on this area, you can improve your ability to be sure that you don't skip over this step. You can fill in the blueprint with a list of pain points that other prospects have shared or have experienced. When you have this list, you can be better prepared when trying to trigger some pain that the prospect is experiencing.

Building Interest Points: There really should be a compartment specifically for building interest. If you don't effectively build interest, you are going to have tough time getting any forward movement. In this compartment, you can have a list of key points that can help to trigger interest from the prospect.

Name Drops: Name dropping is something that you may overlook during the fast pace of a cold call. One way to make sure you get that piece of valuable information into the conversation is to have a compartment in your blueprint for name dropping. To be prepared, you can have a brief list of individuals or businesses that you have worked with and some details around how you have helped them.

Close: Regardless of the goal of the cold call, there should be some sort of close that you are going for. As a result, there could be a compartment of the blueprint where you will focus your attention on closing the prospect on moving on to the next step of the sale cycle. If needed, you can script out some closing language to use at the end of your calls that drives toward the goals that you are working toward.

On the next page an example of putting these compartments together into a plan that can be used as a guide while cold calling:

The Cold Call Blueprint	
Goals of the Call	**Primary:** Schedule a face-to-face or phone appointment. **Secondary:** Get email address and/or organizational information.
Target	**Industry:** Software, Technology **Geography:** US **Company size:** $10 million to $500 million annual revenue **Current state:** Having trouble with producing leads **Title:** VP of Sales, Director of Sales, Owner, CEO
Gatekeeper Introduction	Hi, I am trying to connect with [*insert name or title*]. Can you point me in the right direction?
Prospect Introduction	Hello _____, this is Michael Halper calling from Launch Pad Solutions. Have I caught you in the middle of anything?
Value Statement	We help companies to improve the area of sales revenue and we do this by improving the area of cold calling.
Soft Disqualify	I actually don't know if what we have is a good fit for you so I had just a couple of questions if you have a minute?
Soft Qualifying Questions	▪ How would you rate your sales team's ability to generate leads on a scale from 1 to 10? ▪ What type of sales training programs have your sales resources gone through? ▪ What are your plans for driving improvements in the area of lead generation for the next year? ▪ Are you the right person to speak with about this?
Pain Points	Ok, as we talk with other [*insert title*] what we notice is that they often have concerns with: ▪ Having sales resources that are not able to generate leads ▪ Having difficulty training sales resources ▪ Needing to find a way to create more leads ▪ Wanting to find a way to decrease sales staff turnover Are those things that you can relate to?
Building Interest Points	Based on what you shared, it might be productive for us to talk in more detail. The reason is: ▪ We help to teach sales people to successfully deal with all of the challenges that come with cold calling ▪ We typically see an increase in lead production of between 60 and 80 percent ▪ Our clients often see an increase in overall sales between 10 to 15% ▪ Our techniques and tactics are powerful, yet practical and easy to implement and that is how we differ from the other options available in our space
Name Drops	For example, we worked with GenaTech and trained their inside sales team; they were able to help increase their overall sales by 15%.
Close	Since I have called you out of the blue, I do not want to take any more of your time to talk right now. If you would like to continue this conversation, we can schedule a brief 15 to 20-minute conversation where I can either pop by your office or we can talk on the phone. Is that something you want to put on the calendar?

Blueprint Benefits

Once you have the blueprint in place, you can then use it as a guide while making calls. Of course, the calls might not follow the blueprint exactly, but by at least having a framework and flow to work from, you can likely see many improvements to your cold calling efforts.

Clarity: It is common to not really know what to do and what to say when it is time to pick up the phone and call prospects. But if you have a blueprint to work from, you can flip that 180 degrees and go from confusion to clarity.

Focus: As we have seen by covering the different topics in this book, there are many different things that need to be accomplished during a very brief cold call – you need to communicate value, find pain, qualify, build interest, etc. By having the blueprint broken down into compartments, it will be easier to ensure that you focus on all of the different steps that you need to go through during the call.

Confidence: By having more clarity as to what you will do when the prospect answers the phone, you can greatly improve your confidence while making calls.

Decrease stress: It can be common to experience stress when making cold calls. Part of this can come from not knowing what to say and not being in control of what is going to happen. Having a blueprint can decrease those concerns and this can help to decrease the stress associated with making cold calls.

Improve the impression: By having a blueprint to work from, you will sound more prepared, more intelligent, and more experienced. And all of this will stand to greatly improve the impression that you make with the prospect. You can essentially begin to sound like the polished news anchor that is on the evening news.

Visit www.salesscripter.com to access a tool that will help you to build a custom-tailored blueprint for your products and services.

PRACTICE MAKES PERFECT

Once you have your blueprint in place, it is very helpful to get in some practice with it before you get on the phone with prospects. One of the best ways to practice is to do some form of role-playing where you go through anticipated sales scenarios and work on your messaging and responses.

Through role-playing, you can begin to work through all of the information and knowledge that you need to have your hands around in order to be successful. Getting on the phone without practicing is like putting an athlete in a game who has not practiced or warmed up at all. The more you practice, the better you will be while on the phone.

It can sometimes be difficult to find someone to role-play with. Here are some options to consider when trying to get in some quality practice.

Sales manager: Ask a sales manager to work through a few different scenarios with you.

Team lead: Find a team lead or a senior member of the team to work with.

Sales coach: Working with an external or internal sales coach can be a great forum for role-playing.

Automated software: Visit www.salesscripter.com to access software that will allow you to go through a simulation that enables you to role-play and practice without needed the help of anybody else.

RESEARCH

Performing some sort of research prior to making a cold call can be a helpful step in building out your script. There are three key areas where to perform research: the company, the prospect, and the industry the company is in. Having knowledge in these areas will enable you to make more informed statements and questions and this will not only make your calls more productive, it can also impress the prospect as it will display that you are sharp and you have done your homework.

Here is some direction on what information can be valuable to uncover for the three key research areas.

1. Researching the company

In the old-school world of sales, the sales person might start out a meeting by saying, "Tell me about your business." Prospects today expect you to already know about their business in terms of history, portfolio of products, organizational structure, challenges, etc.

A good place to start to get some of this information is the prospect's website. You can review an "About Us" section on a company's website and can usually find a good summary of the company's history and the road they have traveled. Another good source of information will be a prospect's listing of news articles and press releases. You can try to scan these to see any significant events that the company has announced to learn a little more about their strategy and direction. While reviewing information on a company's website, it is important to be aware that the information may be skewed to how the company wants to be perceived. It is still a good place to gather information to build your understanding on what the company does and the direction they are trying to go. It just might not be the most unbiased source of information.

A company's annual report can be another valuable resource for company information as it will typically provide a great summary of the business environment that the company is operating in and also highlight some insights into overall strategy and direction. You can also analyze some of the financial data in the annual report to find trends or challenges in their business, and these can be very impressive discussion points to bring up during a cold call. Be sure to use some finesse when sharing any negative trends that the prospect might not be proud of.

To gather information that might be less biased, you can simply put the name of the company into search engines to see what type of results and information can be found. Search engines like Google and Yahoo have finance sections to their sites which can be good central places to locate a concentration of valuable company information on the company's stock, financial reports, news, industry, competition, etc. There are also subscription services like Hoovers and OneSource that can provide information similar to the free resources but offer very valuable financial and organizational information.

The amount of research performed per call or per account should have an inverse relationship with the number of accounts that need to be called. In other words, if you have a long list of businesses to cold call, you cannot perform extensive research on each business. But if you are working on a fairly short, finite list of assigned accounts, you should definitely go through some research steps to gather key information before making each call.

2. Researching the actual players

It can be very productive to perform some research on the actual individual whom you are going to be calling. A good process for this would be to put the prospect's name into search engines and social media platforms to see what kind of data can be found. Key pieces of information to look for are details about how the she fits into the organization, her career or previous work history, personal interests, and mutual contacts you may have with her.

These details can not only help you to navigate the organization, but they may also provide valuable points to discuss with the prospect while you are on the phone with her. For example, if you identify that she shares a connection with you, or shares some similar work history, those can be great rapport-building points. If your research on the individual reveals some organizational details, you can use that information to tailor your standard questions to her situation to make the call more productive.

3. Researching the industry

Every business that you want to sell to will be operating inside of an industry and each industry will have its own ecosystem in terms of news, trends, key players, language, politics, etc. Before calling into a target prospect, identify what industry their company falls under and try to increase your level of knowledge about the industry.

Many of the web-based tools that have already been discussed like search engines, Google and Yahoo Finance, and subscription based business information services can be used to gather industry information. There are also industry and trade specific publications and resources that can be used as valuable resources for getting up-to-speed and staying up-to-date on industry specifics.

Similar to the amount of research that you want to do for each account, the amount of research that you should perform for each industry will depend on the number of industries that your target prospects fall into. If you only sell to businesses that fall under one industry, you should try to submerse yourself into learning as much as you can about that particular industry. You should know all of the trends, the language, competitive landscape, the latest news, etc. On the other extreme, if you sell to businesses that span across many different industries, you may be limited to only skimming the surface when trying to increase your industry knowledge.

14

INNER GAME

IMPROVING YOUR MENTAL STATE

Whether you think you can or think you can't,
you are right.

Henry Ford

In addition to building your strategy, knowledge, and tools for cold calling, you can also go through some steps to prepare and improve your mental state. This is an important step because sales and cold calling can be very challenging and taxing mentally. Not only will you stand to face rejection from prospects, but you also might face pressure and expectations in terms of results and performance from your employer, and these two factors combined can create a fairly tense environment. This is why finding a way to create a strong mental state is fairly important to not only being successful, but also to have the stamina to deal with the ups and downs.

DISMISS THREE COMMON SALES MYTHS

As a first step to improve your mental state, let's dismiss three important sales myths.

Myth #1 – You should enjoy cold calling

The first myth to dismiss is that you should enjoy cold calling if you are a true sales person. This is not something that you hear sales managers preaching; rather, it is implied on the basis that cold calling is typically part of every sales position, and there is the expectation that you should enjoy your job if you have chosen the right profession.

This myth needs to be dismissed because just about everyone has a little reluctance to making cold calls. This is driven by the fact that we face the potential for rejection with every cold call that we make and it is natural to dislike the feeling of rejection.

By dismissing this sales myth and becoming more aware that the negative feelings toward cold calling are natural and something that everybody has, you can begin to improve your mental state by being assured that you are normal and have everything you need to be successful.

Myth #2 – You are born a sales person

The next sales myth that we need to dismiss is that you are born a sales person and you either have the genetic makeup to be successful or you don't. There are plenty of sales managers out there who still operate with this belief, and the main challenge with this is that it takes some of the power out of your hands in terms of your ability to improve your sales skills and results. If it is your genetic makeup that determines how good a sales person you can be, then all you can do is hope that you have the right genes.

It is important to point out that there is a little truth in this myth, as our biological makeup does influence our capacity to learn and also dictates our personality traits and tendencies. And these qualities can impact how good at sales someone will or will not be. For example, if someone does not have the capacity to learn, then he might not be able to learn and grasp all of the information that he will need to know in order to successfully sell. In addition, if a person has an extremely introverted personality that makes him incapable of interacting with people he does not know, he will clearly have a tough time selling.

But this perception that you are born a sales person is primarily based on the premise that someone must have a particular personality type and level of competitiveness in order to be able to sell. This is where this myth becomes flawed. To begin to break this down, your level of competitiveness can develop and change throughout your life depending on your environment and what you are taught. You definitely either want to have or hire someone with a high level of desire, drive, competitiveness, and ambition because those qualities influence success. But these are not necessarily qualities that someone is born with—they can be acquired and developed throughout one's life.

Moving on to the personality factor: Personalities of all different types can be present in successful sales people. Many believe that the "gift of gab," or a very talkative personality, is a requirement or key factor in someone being a successful sales person. Of course, if you are interacting with prospects and customers, you have to be able to interact and communicate with strangers at an effective level. But there is no need for sales people to be extreme extroverts or the loudest people in the room. In fact, in professional business-to-business selling, the ability to listen is almost a more important skill than talking.

The main point with dismissing this sales myth is that if someone has the desire and capacity to learn, has the desire and competitive fire to win and succeed, and has the ability to communicate on a professional level, then he has what it takes to be a successful sales person, regardless of the genetic code he is born with.

Myth #3 – A true sales person will be a good cold caller

Following on the previous two myths is the myth that a true sales person should be a good cold caller. This is a myth because there are a lot mechanics to effective cold calling, and as a result, not only can a great sales person could be a sub-par cold caller by not being sharp on the minor tactics, but also that someone with little sales knowledge or experience could be an excellent cold caller.

This myth is important to be aware of to improve and maintain a strong mental state as cold calling can be very challenging and this can cause doubt. When we face this doubt, we can become confused because, while we believe that we are a good sales person, we may have trouble when it comes to producing results from cold calling.

The reality is that not only can just about everybody use a little training and help with getting better at cold calling, but more importantly, cold calling is a low-success-rate activity. That means that regardless of how good you are and how well you perform, you are going to have fewer cold calls that go well than ones that appear to be unsuccessful. In other words, if you make ten conversations while cold calling, it would be understandable to only have two or three good conversations, even if you are executing at an optimum level.

This is similar to how a baseball player who has a batting average around .300 is considered to be an excellent player. They get on base only three times out of every ten attempts. That is a low number but if you understand the sport, you know that it is hitting the ball and getting on base is a difficult thing to do. The same relationship applies to cold calling, as there are many factors in play and a fairly small sweet spot that we are trying to hit.

Once you stop to dismiss those three myths, you can begin to strengthen your confidence and mental state. Although, you still may have some resistance and reluctance to jumping on the phone to make calls, and we will begin to dig into that next.

APPROACH ANXIETY

Regardless of your years of experience, it is likely that you sometimes dread making cold calls. If cold calling is fairly easy from an energy investment level—pick up the phone, dial a number, and run through a script—why is it that you can dread doing it so much? The answer to that question can be traced back to a concept called approach anxiety.

Approach anxiety is the feeling that people experience when they are considering approaching somebody they do not know. This could occur in a number of different scenarios, but the most common would be where a man is interested in talking to woman he does not know. In this scenario, this man may feel fear and a pit in his stomach before he approaches the woman. In many cases, this feeling can be so intense that it prevents him from approaching the person he is interested in. The anxiety can be very intense, yet the worst outcome that can occur is rejection from a complete stranger who will probably never be seen again.

The explanation of this fear and this anxiety is that we as humans extremely dislike the feeling of rejection. According to Maslow's hierarchy of needs, a theory in psychology, proposed by Abraham Maslow in his 1943 paper *A Theory of Human Motivation*, Maslow outlines five levels of core needs that drive human behavior and decision making. One of the levels of needs is labeled as Love and Belonging, and this is where we have a need to feel a sense of belonging and acceptance. This is the area of our basic needs that makes it us feel like we need to belong, to fit in, and to be accepted by those that we interact with. Whether we are with close family and friends, we are at work, we are participating in a sporting activity, at a professional organization, or maybe at a purely social event, we have an internal desire to have the people we are interacting with like and approve us.

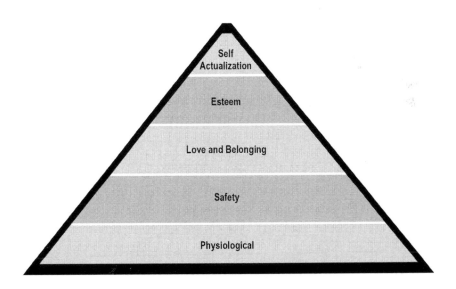

This is a pretty important need for us, as it falls right after our need for security and safety. In other words, it is almost as important to us that people accept us as it is for people to not physically attack us. As a result, when we experience rejection, we take a fairly negative hit in this area of core needs, and this can cause us significant emotional and mental discomfort. To avoid this mental pain, we consciously and subconsciously avoid situations where we may experience rejection.

Just as approach anxiety can affect and prevent a man from approaching a woman, it can affect and prevent a sales person from cold calling. Even though the worst thing that can happen is for someone to say they aren't interested or hang up on us, this potential outcome can create approach anxiety and create resistance and dread when it comes time to start cold calling.

If you can relate to this feeling and you can see the potential connection with approach anxiety, the first step to effectively dealing with or decreasing it is to simply become more aware of what it is and why it occurs. After that, there are some very clear things that you can do to decrease this anxiety and those are explained throughout the remainder of this chapter.

PREPARATION

One way to improve your mental state and decrease any anxiety is to be better prepared. Think about when you were in school and you took a test you were not prepared for as much as you wanted to be. Did you feel stressed and maybe a little anxiety? Now compare that with an instance where you knew the information inside and out. Did you have more confidence and comfort when you were completely prepared?

Being prepared for cold calls can give you that same comfort and confidence. This could include having a script, knowing your product, knowing your customer, knowing your competition, and preparing for the objections you are likely to receive.

VALUE AWARENESS

One thing that you can do to improve your mental state is to go through a process where you reflect on all of the value that you have to offer the prospects you are calling. This reflection can make you more aware of how you help and can improve your level of confidence while decreasing anxiety and reluctance.

The reason that this reflection is important is that we have products and services that we need to sell. And we need to close sales not only because we likely have sales targets and quotas looming over our heads, but also because we likely have bills to pay and families to provide for. With those factors being involved, we can easily have these needs at the front of our minds when we are cold calling. This can put us in a needy mental state and frame of mind. We basically need the prospect to buy something from us and this state of mind can have a very negative impact on how we interact with prospects.

But if we stop to think about all the great ways that our products help our existing clients, if we also think about all of the great qualities of our company, and we then add in all of the great experience and knowledge that we bring to the table, we can then reach a place where all of the value that we have to offer is at the front of our thoughts. This shift in thoughts can improve your mental state.

SALES AFFIRMATIONS

One exercise to use to help build value awareness and strengthen positive thoughts is to use sales affirmations. Sales affirmations are a list of positive qualities and attributes that you have to offer. The following are a few examples of positive statements that can be built specific to each person and used as a key tool to improve and maintain a strong mental state.

- Our services have helped our past clients to increase sales by 15% consistently.
- Our products are designed better and last longer than any of our competitors.
- Businesses desperately need the services that we provide.

When you write or type out statements like this on a piece of paper, you can then use that as an exercise and tool to improve your mental strength. As part of your daily warm up activities, you can read over the list to remind yourself of the positive points. It can be very helpful if the list of sales affirmations can be printed out and posted somewhere where you will see them and read them from time-to-time while on the phone making cold calls.

Why Affirmations Help

When you get knocked down during cold calling by people being rude and rejecting your interest in talking with them, you can easily begin to doubt yourself and the products or services you sell. This doubt can have a negative impact on performance, as it can increase reluctance for future cold call activity: Why should I cold call if nobody wants to buy anything? The other thing that the doubt can do is impact your presence when communicating to prospects, as the doubt can create a lack of confidence, and this can be heard in your tonality and what you say.

Sales affirmations help turn you around from the direction of doubt to the direction of confidence. The end result is less resistance and reluctance to reaching out to prospects, which can have a positive impact on activity levels. In addition, these can help us to increase your level of confidence and that can give off a much more powerful and impressive presence when talking with prospects.

What are Good Affirmations?

If your goal is to use these statements to improve and strengthen your mental state, then you want them to be as strong and positive as possible. Yet they should also be true and realistic statements that you can stand behind and believe in, because if you do not truly believe the affirmation or declaration, then it might have little impact on strengthening your mental state.

Below are some areas to think about when making affirmations.

Affirmations about you: Just about everybody has strengths and certain things that they do well. As part of building affirmations, think about all of the good qualities that you bring to the table.

- I operate with integrity and prospects notice and appreciate that
- Due to my experience and knowledge, prospects see me as a trusted advisor
- I am good at communicating and building rapport with prospects

Affirmations about what you are selling: In most cases, what you are selling will deliver some sort of value and benefit to your prospects. Build affirmations that focus on the strengths regarding what you sell.

- Our products have an ROI that provides a payback of 12 months
- Our services help companies to stay in business
- Businesses that don't use our services are losing money due to errors and compliance risks

Affirmations about the organization that you represent: Every market has fierce competition. When you are in the trenches fighting against these competitors and sometimes losing deals, it can be easy to lose confidence in the organization and company that you work for. Build a list of the great things about your organization and the advantages that you have against the competition.

- Our processes are better than all of our competitors
- We have been doing this longer than any other company
- We offer the best level of customer service and support

ROUTINE

Getting into some sort of routine with making cold calls can also help to improve your mental state and decrease cold call anxiety. Here's an example of how a routine can help: Consider a sales person starting her day. She starts out not wanting to make cold calls. A routine that may decrease her anxiety is to go over some affirmations, review some product and customer information, outline some notes on what she is going to discuss, and then make some warm calls to lower levels or to people that are more approachable. From there, she can build some momentum and transition to some power prospecting time that is focused trying to connect with more challenging "high value targets". This type of routine can help you to warm up, defuse anxiety, and improve your mental state.

Another way to incorporate a routine is to actually schedule time with yourself to make cold calls by putting aside a block of hours during the week when you will shut everything else down and power out some calls. When you use a tactic like this, not only will you be better prepared mentally when it is time to get on the phone by clearly shifting gears and getting into the right mode, but it also creates an increased level of accountability with yourself.

DEALING WITH REJECTION

You are guaranteed to encounter some form of rejection when making cold calls. It is simply part of the job. There are a few things you can keep in mind regarding rejection to help you maintain a strong mental state.

Not personal: You need to keep in mind that when someone says "no" and rejects your cold call, he is rejecting the call attempt and not you as a person. It is nothing personal as he will not likely know who you are or anything about you. This may sound silly to point out, but it is common to react to rejection on a cold call by taking it personally in some way.

No physical pain: There is not any physical pain that can result from cold call rejection. The worst thing that can happen is getting hung up on.

Not everybody is a fit: If you are calling to sell a product, there is no possible way that everybody that you call is going to be a qualified prospect. As a result, you will have to get rejection when you encounter some of the prospects who are simply not a fit for what you sell.

Still accomplishing something: When someone rejects you, it may hurt and feel like you are wasting your time. But the reality is that even when someone hangs up on you or says "no," you are still accomplishing something, as you can now take that person off your list of people to call. Every "no" gets you one step closer to a "yes."

15

ACTIVITY

GETTING IN THE GAME

*Some people want it to happen, some wish it
would happen, others make it happen.*

MICHAEL JORDAN

One variable of the Cold Calling Equation that needs mentioning, but probably not that much explanation or analysis, is the variable of activity. In order for any of the other variables in the equation to take effect, you have to get on the phone at some point, and there are a few things you can do to maintain consistent cold calling activity levels.

Even if you are absolutely determined to hit the phones when the week starts, there are two consistent factors that will likely stand in your way. First, there is the natural resistance and reluctance to get on the phone. But

THE COLD CALLING EQUATION

another factor that can throw a wrench in your plans is the likelihood that cold calling is just one of many sales activities that you must take care of. You might also be responsible for activities like taking care of existing customers, working on existing leads and opportunities, performing administrative tasks, attending recurring training, etc.

Not only is it easy for other stuff to get in the way of cold calling, but when we have a little reluctance to getting on the phone, we can usually find something else to do that is more important at that particular moment. For example, we might choose to work on some paperwork that needs to be completed when it is time to hit the phones. The paperwork is important and needs to be taken care of, and when we skip out on the cold calling for another important activity, we feel less guilty and can use this to justify our decision to not make calls. This is an example of being "productively unproductive," as we are still being productive but we are not being productive in one area that needs attention. If we skip over making calls and never go back to make sure it gets the needed time and attention, we can expect to see a negative impact on our activity level.

SCHEDULE TIME

We discussed in Chapter 14 how scheduling time with yourself to make cold calls can help improve your mental state. You can also use this same tactic to decrease the call reluctance and minimize the possibility of finding other work to do instead of making calls. This would involve using some system to allocate a portion of the day or week for time where you shut down everything else and focus solely on making calls.

What this can look like is to physically put a few one- to two-hour long blocks on your calendar for time that is dedicated to cold calling, and have those recur every week. If you are diligent about keeping those appointments with yourself, you will typically see an increase in cold calling activity.

DECREASE MULTITASKING

Another tactic that you can use to increase cold calling activity is to decrease multitasking when it is time to make calls. This is worth attention because we have become a society that is pretty much currently in a hyper-multitasking mode.

A common environment for a sales person can include a steadily flow of disruptions and distractions from email, mobile phone, office phone, text messages, internet, social media, and more. This can create noise and that can slow down or halt your cold calling activity. If you are able to decrease the noise by eliminating the multitasking during your scheduled cold calling time, you can greatly increase your activity levels. To eliminate even the temptation of distraction, close your email down, turn off your cell phone, and close any social media accounts that you are logged into.

SET TARGETS AND TRACK PROGRESS

Setting goals and targets is crucial to being successful in all aspects of sales. Increasing cold calling activity is another area where goals and targets can have a direct impact on results. If you set targets in terms of the amount of call time, number of dials, number of hits, and number of appointments for the day or week, you are much more likely to have higher activity levels than if you just worked with no clear end point.

Along with defining what you are trying to achieve, there is also some power in the actual act of tracking the progress you are making against your targets and goals. Not only is this important for simply knowing where you are in terms of tracking toward your goals or targets, but the act of tracking and viewing progress can actually produce a strong feeling of accomplishment, and this can help to not only fuel some momentum, but it can also defuse any cold calling anxiety that might exist.

16

VOICE

COMMUNICATING EFFECTIVELY

The human voice is the organ of the soul.

HENRY WADSWORTH LONGFELLOW

When talking with someone in person, the majority of how we communicate is through our body language. While we put a lot of emphasis on what we say, it is really our facial expression, posture, and hand gestures that communicates the most to people we are interacting with. After body language, the tonality that we use in terms of how we say what we say is the second most impactful way that we communicate. And coming in third behind those two are the words that we choose to say.

How that applies to communicating over the phone is that you remove the factor of body language. As a result, your tonality and how you say what you say becomes one of the most important factors in how you communicate.

SENDING OUT GOOD VIBES

The sub-communications that you produce through your tonality can have a major impact on the vibes that you are sending out to the prospect. By the simple way that you say something, a prospect can pick up on a particular vibe, and that can influence whether she has a positive or negative image of you.

To illustrate this, the following table lists out negative vibes that you can easily, and sometimes subconsciously, send out to prospects you talk to on the phone. On the right side of that table is a corresponding list for the positive counterpart for each negative vibe.

Once you have that list side by side, you can not only see a summary of some of the negative vibes that you might be subconsciously sending out, but also see a very positive list of corresponding vibes that you could consciously try to send out in place of the negative ones by focusing on changing and improving your voice.

Negative Vibes	Positive Vibes
Nervous	Confident
Cold	Warm
Abrasive	Easy going
Irritated	Calm
Needy	Abundance
Inexperienced	Experienced
Aggressive	Passive
Unintelligent	Intelligent
Unfriendly	Friendly
Self-absorbed	Serving
Dishonest	Honest

Negative Vibes

To understand the power of spending some thought and attention in this area, let's look at the potential thoughts that the prospect might be thinking when we accidentally send some of these negative vibes.

Vibe Given Off	Prospect's Perception of the Sales Person
Nervous	▪ He is not experienced ▪ He does not know what he is doing ▪ He might not be credible ▪ It might be uncomfortable to work with him
Cold	▪ He is not very nice ▪ I do not want to help this sales person ▪ It might be uncomfortable to work with him
Abrasive	▪ He is not easy to talk to ▪ I do not want to work with this person ▪ I do not want to help this person
Irritated	▪ He must not be very good at his job ▪ He must not have a good product to sell ▪ I do not want to work with this person ▪ I do not want to help this person
Needy	▪ He must not be selling very much ▪ He must not have a good product to sell ▪ He is going to bug me a lot
Inexperienced	▪ He might not know what he is talking about ▪ He might not be credible ▪ It might be uncomfortable to work with him
Aggressive	▪ He is difficult to talk to ▪ I do not want to work with this person ▪ He is going to bug me a lot ▪ I do not want to help this person
Unintelligent	▪ He might not be good at his job ▪ He might not be credible ▪ It might be uncomfortable to work with him
Unfriendly	▪ He is difficult to talk to ▪ He is unpleasant to work with ▪ I do not want to work with this person ▪ I do not want to help this person
Self-absorbed	▪ I do not know if I can trust this person ▪ This person does not care about me ▪ I do not want to help this person
Dishonest	▪ I do not know if I can trust this person ▪ He might not be credible ▪ I do not want to work with this person ▪ I do not want to help this person

The take away from this list is that sub-communicating any of these vibes to a gatekeeper or prospect can decrease her motivation to help you, to work with you, and to buy your products and services.

Positive Vibes

As we already pointed out, each negative vibe has a positive counterpart. Going through the same exercise, if you improved your tonality to eliminate any negative vibes and replace them with their positive counterparts, you could anticipate some of the thoughts and feelings that are that detailed in the table on next page.

As you can see, if you are able to shift from giving off negative vibes to giving off positive vibes by modifying your tonality, you can greatly improve your ability to establish conversations and relationships with prospects.

IMPROVING TONALITY

After looking at the impacts from giving off negative and positive vibes, one might be motivated to learn about what to do to avoid giving off negative vibes. But we will go about it another way and focus more on ways to give off positive vibes.

Don't Worry, Be Happy

What we can often overlook is that our internal feelings and moods can easily be displayed to others through our tonality when we speak. With that being the case, you can sometimes listen to the way somebody says something and pick up on how they feel at that particular time.

Applying this to cold calling, if you are nervous, unhappy, or don't feel like making sales calls, it can likely be heard on the other end of the phone, and this could establish a poor start to a cold call. On the flip side of this, if you are excited about what you are doing and thoroughly enjoy it, that feeling will be communicated through your voice while talking over the phone, and this can have a very positive impact on how you are received by the person on the other end of the phone.

Vibe Given Off	Prospect's Perception of the Sales Person
Confident	▪ He must know what he is doing ▪ He might be credible ▪ I will like working with him
Warm	▪ He is nice ▪ I want to help this sales person ▪ I will like working with him
Easy going	▪ He is easy to talk to ▪ He is pleasant to work with ▪ I will like working with him
Calm	▪ He must be good at his job ▪ Maybe that is because he has a good product to sell ▪ He will be easy to work with ▪ I want to help this person
Abundance	▪ He must be selling a lot ▪ He must have a good product to sell ▪ He is not going to be bugging me
Experienced	▪ He knows what he is talking about ▪ He might be credible ▪ I will like working with him
Passive	▪ He is easy to talk to ▪ He is pleasant to work with ▪ He is not going to bug me a lot
Intelligent	▪ He might be good at his job ▪ He might know what he is talking about ▪ He might be credible ▪ I will like working with him
Friendly	▪ He is easy to talk to ▪ He is fun to work with ▪ I want to work with this person ▪ I want to help this person
Serving	▪ I think I trust this person ▪ This person seems to care about me ▪ I want to help this person
Honest	▪ I think I can trust this person ▪ I want to work with this person ▪ I want to help this person

But how often do we really get thrilled about or enjoy making cold calls? One trick to use here to make it sound like you are enjoying making calls even if you are not is to physically grin or smile while talking on the phone – smile and dial. Even though the prospect cannot see you, implementing this simple body language change will actually make you sound happier and friendlier over the phone by improving your tonality.

Another tactic that can help to make you happier to improve how you sound is to go through some of the mental inner game exercises discussed in Chapter 14 on Inner Game. By going through affirmations and becoming more aware of the value that you hold and have to offer, you can stand to improve your tonality and the vibes that you communicate while on the phone.

Tactics to help: sales affirmations, value awareness, warm-up calling, smiling while on the phone

Potential vibes and impression: confident, warm, easy going, abundance, friendly, serving

Effectively Displaying Confidence

One of the easiest ways to give off positive vibes is to sound confident in your voice. The challenge here is that it can be pretty easy to lose a little confidence when cold calling. We face frequent reject since the person on the other end of the phone can ultimately choose whether to let the call get established. But if you truly believe in your products, in your company, and in the value that you offer, then you should be able to carry yourself with a high level of confidence and have that communicate through your voice.

Tactics to help: sales affirmations, value awareness, role-playing, preparation

Potential vibes and impression: confident, abundance, experienced, intelligent, credible

Communicating with Curiosity

As we discussed in Chapter 8 on dealing with gatekeepers, one tactic to use with a gatekeeper is to try to enlist his help while trying to get him on your side. And one way to do this is by modifying your tonality to sound a bit lost and curious. This can be a tone that expresses that you don't know exactly whom you need to talk to and that you could use help being pointed in the right direction.

One way to sound curious and in need of help is to use a tone and inflection that adds a question mark to sentences that aren't questions. The following is an example of turning very direct statement into more of a question, creating a tonality that invites help and information.

"Please connect me with the human resources manager."

"I am trying to connect with the human resources manager?"

This statement is delivered with an inflection that is curious or perplexed. From there, a direct question asking for the gatekeeper's help in figuring out whom to speak with or what direction to go can be delivered. This tactic can help to improve your ability to work with gatekeepers.

Tactics to help: talk with a curious tone, add a question mark to the end of statements

Potential vibes and impression: warm, soft, easy going, friendly, honest

Sound like You Don't Need the Deal

One way to greatly improve the way you sound over the phone and give off positive vibes is to sound like you don't need the deal. The two extremes of the impression that can be made with a prospect are a sales person who hasn't sold anything for a while and is worried about keeping his job and, on the other extreme, a sales person who has a line of prospects who are ready to purchase and is almost indifferent as to whether the prospect purchases or not. There is a tremendous difference between how a prospect perceives these two different sales people, and you can improve your results by using tonality that presents you as a sales person who has abundance rather than a lack of solid prospects.

The reality is that we likely fall in the middle of that spectrum, always being a little needy and wanting to close the prospects that we talk to. But what is more important than how we truly feel is the impression that we are giving off to prospects. If we give off the impression that we "need" the deal, which is different than showing that we "want" the deal, we are not only sub-communicating fairly negative vibes about our experience, our credibility, and the quality of our products and services, but we are also giving up some power when it comes time to negotiate.

The best way to sound like you don't need the deal is to present yourself in the same way that you would if you had already hit and exceeded your sales targets. If you carry yourself like you are above plan and in a very comfortable position in terms of sales and pipeline, this will come through in your tonality and create a more positive impression with prospects. You will always know how badly you want and need the deal, but if you at least act like you don't necessarily need the deal, you will present yourself as very confident to the prospect. Moreover, if you do that long enough, you may actually begin to trick yourself into creating real confidence that does not need to be faked.

Tactics to help: talk like you are above quota, disqualify the prospect, move forward on prospect's terms

Potential vibes and impression: confident, abundance, experienced, intelligent, credible

17

CONNECT

GETTING A HOLD OF PROSPECTS

Things do not happen. Things are made to happen.
JOHN F. KENNEDY

We have discussed a lot of different tactics that can help you when you are on a cold call with a prospect. But those will not do you much good if you cannot get the prospect on phone. And unfortunately, with changes in technology and other trends working against us, it has become increasingly difficult to get a hold of prospects.

WHY CONNECTING IS DIFFICULT

In some ways, connecting and just getting a hold of prospects will be one of your biggest challenges and this is due to some very basic and understandable factors.

Prospects are Busy

If you are calling prospects at work, it is very safe to assume that they will be fairly busy at the time that you are calling. In today's business environment, prospects are wearing more hats than ever and this can create an environment that is very fast-paced and chaotic. This busyness can definitely impact a prospect's willingness and ability to pick up the phone when you call.

Another factor working against you is that your prospect might be away from their desk most of the day. If you are calling mid-level managers and above, they can often have their calendar filled with meetings most of the day or even be out of the office traveling. Forget whether or not the prospect wants to take your call, if he is never sitting by his phone when you call, it is going to be very difficult to connect.

Let's stop to think about a prospect that has been in meetings or traveling and that finally gets a chance to be back at his desk. This individual is likely going to be extremely busy catching up on items that were missed while he was away. If you are able to time it just right so that you call when this busy prospect is at his desk, he may ignore your call based solely on the fact that he simply cannot take a call from being away and being too busy.

Tremendous Competition

Another factor to be aware of is that there is a tremendous amount of competition that you face from other sales people calling the same prospects that you are trying to reach. Especially if you are calling at a decision maker level; everybody is trying to reach the individuals that have the power to make decisions and approve purchases. And that is not just limited to your direct competitors as you also have to compete with sales people that sell products that have nothing to do with your particular space.

What this competition means to you is that your prospect's phone might get a high volume of calls throughout the day and this can make your job of trying to connect more difficult. The reason this has an impact is that the prospect cannot answer every call as he would be on the phone all day talking to vendors. And if there is the conscious acknowledgement that some calls must be ignored in order to stay productive, your call could easily be chosen to be one of the ignored calls.

Gatekeepers

As discussed in Chapter 8 on dealing with gatekeepers, in order to avoid sales calls, prospects will often create it so that you will have to go through a gatekeeper in order to get to them. There are some things you can do to minimize the challenges that gatekeepers present, but at the end of the day, gatekeepers contribute to the difficulty involved with trying to connect with prospects.

Automated Attendants

We also discussed automated attendants in Chapter 8 and how they are another form of gatekeeper that we face. When outlining the challenges that stand in your way of connecting with prospects, these deserve a mention all to their own as they are becoming increasingly more common and many are downright impossible to get through if you do not know exactly whom you are trying to reach. Auto-attendants play a very big role in the increasing challenge of connecting with prospects.

As you can see, simply connecting can be fairly challenging. These factors are what they are and there is noting that we can do to change any of those. What we can do is find a way to work around and minimize the challenges and that is what we will focus on for the remainder of this chapter.

CALL CADENCE

One thing that you do have control over is when you call the prospect and how many times you call. And this can be referred to as your call cadence. Another word for cadence is rhythm, and you can think of this as the rhythm that you use for how much time you will leave between your call attempts.

There is no exact best way to handle this and the call cadence will vary being impacted by industry, the type of prospect being contacted, and possibly the sales person's own personal style. But even though the right answer here can differ, there are some factors to consider when deciding how to handle.

Call Frequency

In order to improve the probability of getting a hold of a prospect, it can help to have a fairly tight circle of repetitive call attempts. In other words, it is better to call the prospect daily or multiple times per day for a few days in a row versus calling the prospect once per week for a few weeks in a row. This tight focus can either help to improve the odds of catching the prospect when he is at his desk, or it may help to motivate the prospect to pick up the phone if he is ignoring your call and recognizes that you have called a couple of times.

When you read the suggestion to call daily or multiple times per day, you may have a question or concern around annoying the prospect by calling too much. The key here is that you have the green light to keep calling as long as you do not speak to anybody or leave any messages. This includes leaving a voicemail message, leaving your information with a gatekeeper, or briefly talking to the prospect. When any of those events occur, there needs to be a grace period of time where you do not call back to avoid creating a negative impression. The length of time that you need to wait will vary but it can be typically range from a couple of days to one week. If you call back during this grace period, you may stand to give off a negative impression and damage the level of rapport. But if there is not a message left and someone were to notice your call attempts, you will just look a little persistent and that is OK. As long as it is not a call every hour and five calls or more per day.

Leaving Voicemail Messages

From what we just described, there is a little more freedom to keep calling back when you do not leave a message. As a result, there can be some advantages to having a call cadence that avoids leaving messages for the most part as you can be more persistent with calling back. You also save a little time from not leaving messages as all of the time talking to voicemail boxes can add up if you are making a large number of cold calls.

Although, when someone never appears to answer their phone, at some point it can be good to use a voicemail message to improve your ability to connect. One way to handle this is to keep calling the prospect but leave a voicemail every five to ten attempts. Once you leave a voicemail message, you might then need to hold off for a few days to one week before you call back.

MULTI-TOUCH

One very effective tactic to help increase your connect rate is to have a multi-touch approach. This is a strategy that incorporates using multiple communication methods to try to successfully connect with the prospect. For example, in addition to using the phone to try to connect, you can incorporate tools such as email, physical mail, and voicemail.

A multi-touch approach can improve your connect rate due to a couple of factors. First, you are going to create a pattern of repetition where the prospect is receiving and seeing your information at different times. This can create a process where your messages start to reinforce one another when your prospect sees them come in. And this approach can provide a layer of redundancy that helps to keep you covered if one of your messages gets completely missed.

Another reason that a multi-touch approach can help is that most people have a preferred way of communicating. Some people prefer to communicate via email and for those, your phone calls might have a low probability of getting through. Others may be the opposite and get so much email that a message to them goes into a black hole and the only real way to get through is to catch with a phone call. Whatever the case, when you use multiple methods of communication, you increase your probability of communicating with the prospect in her preferred communication format.

ORGANIZATIONAL MOVEMENT

Up until this point, we have discussed some ways to improve your ability to connect and get a hold of the prospect. But at the end of the day, there will be some cases where you will not be able to get through, regardless of what you do. When this is the case, one thing you can do is to try to get in through other areas of the organization and you can use a process of organizational movement to help add some logic to how you handle this.

Organizational movement refers to the act of moving on to other internal contacts when you reach a point where it appears that you cannot get a hold of your target prospect. To make this simple, there are two types of organizational movement: vertical and horizontal.

Vertical Organizational Movement

When you feel stuck or at a dead-end when calling a prospect, one of your next actions can be to call other individuals that are in your target prospect's organization or department. For example, you can call individuals that are above your target prospect in the organization and maybe start with the person that the target prospect reports to. Or you could call individuals that are below the target prospect in the organization and maybe start with the person that reports to the target prospect. This is basically moving up and down the organization to try to find a way in and can be referred to as vertical organizational movement.

An example of what vertical organizational movement might look like is one where we are trying to reach the IT director. We get pretty hard screening from the IT director's gatekeeper or we just get a voicemail box every time we call. We have tried some multi-touch techniques and are not getting any responses. At this point, we can shift and try to either call the VP of IT (person the IT director reports to) or we can call the IT manager (direct report to the IT director).

Horizontal Organizational Movement

In addition to moving vertically inside the prospect's department or immediate organization, you can also move horizontally by calling into other departments. The other departments that it might make sense to call into will vary from sales person to sales person. But for most products, there are usually a couple of different departments that are impacted by the purchase and use of what is being sold.

If we pick up with the previous example again of trying to reach an IT director, we are trying to reach IT because we sell project management software. When our software is implemented, the department of Operations is greatly improved with better planning. As a result, it can be very productive to use horizontal movement and shift to calling into Operations when we are not able to connect with prospects in IT.

And while simply connecting can often be the most difficult part of the process and sometimes seem impossible, if you apply a call cadence that applies focus on the prospect, you utilize a multi-touch approach that hits the prospect from different angles, and you move vertically and horizontally throughout the organization, you can optimize and improve your ability to connect and get in.

18

EMAIL

ACCELERATE YOUR RESULTS

*I hear and I forget. I see and I remember.
I do and I understand.*

CONFUCIUS

With it becoming increasingly difficult to get prospects on the phone, it is key to have a strategy for how to utilize email as a way to communicate and get a prospect's attention.

EMAIL FUNDAMENTALS

Each sales person's situation is unique and this makes it difficult to say exactly how you should build your prospecting email messages. Although, there are some basic fundamentals that can apply to just about every situation and taking these into consideration can often improve your effectiveness.

Focus on the Right Goal

And remember, just as our goal of your cold call is more to create a conversation with the prospect than to sell your product, the same applies to your email. The email should open the door and trigger interest in talking. It does not need to fully explain what you do and get the prospect to want to purchase or confirm that he needs what you have to offer.

Use Brevity

You likely have a lot that you want to say in the emails that you want send to a prospect, but it is important to be fairly brief in your messages. Remember that the prospects that you are trying to reach are very busy and they are also getting calls and emails from other sales people. As result, prospects are not likely to read long, verbose messages.

Another reason to use brevity when writing emails to your prospects is that you do not want to give them too much information. If you get crafty with your message and don't provide all the details around what you are all about, you may create a little curiosity and that can help grab the prospect's attention. Another reason to not give too much information is that, if you fully list out what you provide, the prospect can scan the list and make the decision that they do not need you without even giving you an opportunity to have a conversation.

Focus on Value and Pain

One way to be brief, yet still create powerful messages, is to incorporate points around the value you offer and the pain you resolve. Focusing in these areas can help to grab the prospect's attention and you can reserve some of the more detailed information for your first conversation with the prospect.

This approach also helps to keep you from going in the natural direction of wanting to talk too much about your products and services. When it comes to email, or even talking on the phone, it is very common to want to talk about all the great things that you products and company can do. This is a very "all about me" approach. When you focus your messages on value, and pain, you will be using an approach that is more "all about you".

Make Emails Look One-to-One

In order to improve your efficiency and reach when sending emails, you may start using email templates and sending mass email blasts. If you do use tools like this, one tactic that can help to improve getting your emails read and responded to is to make your mass emails look like they were written one at a time and specifically for the prospect that is receiving it.

The logic behind this is that if your email looks like a mass email that has been sent out to a large number of recipients, it is much more likely to get viewed as spam and ignored or deleted unread. A prospect will be more willing to stop and spend his time to read your email if he thinks that you stopped to spend time to write the email specifically for him. If he gets a hint that your email was a mass email, not only will he not feel bad about ignoring it, he will feel confident that he is not missing anything important since it was a blast versus a one-to-one message. As result, design your emails so they appear one-to-one and not one-to-many.

Here are a few very simple things you can do to make your email templates appear more like a one-to-one message. And a quick disclaimer, these are tactics when sending "sales" emails to prospects to compliment and improve your cold calling. If you are sending more "marketing" emails and you do not care as much about the one-to-many impression, the below should not be applied.

1. Avoid graphics and images

If your email has graphics and images like pictures, banners, or borders, this is basically telling the recipient, "I designed this fancy looking email and I am sending it to a lot of different people." If you do the opposite of that and use a very plain email with little to no cosmetic formatting, the prospect will be more likely to think that it is a one-to-one email and give it a little more attention.

Another way to look at this point is to consider the routine of going through your physical mail at home. You may quickly tear up and throw away the pieces of mail that you are able to identify as being a mass mail piece that has been sent to a lot of different people. But think about what you do when you come across an envelope that has your address written out by hand. When you see this, you may be more likely to stop to open and closely examine what the piece of mail is as someone must have taken some time to send you something.

2. Avoid hyperlinks

A very common practice in marketing emails and on websites is the act of inserting hyperlinks. Hyperlinks are links that are produced when you highlight a set of words and then link them to a webpage. This is a very effective tactic to use to lead a prospect to additional information. Although, when you include hyperlinks in the body of your email templates, it can give off the impression that the message is a mass email and one-to-many.

Think about what a sales person that is making a number of calls and sending a number of one-to-one emails might do, or not do. She might skip taking the time to put crafty hyperlinks in her message. While putting these links in a message is fairly easy to do, more often than not, a busy sales person may skip that step and just stick a full link in an email instead of taking the extra step to create a clean hyperlink.

Including hyperlinks is not horrible, but they can slightly increase the potential for giving off a mass email impression. If you want to direct the prospect to a webpage, one option is to just copy and paste the whole URL into your message.

3. Use a personal salutation

Use a personal salutation in your email like "Hi [first name]" or "Hello [first name]". This by itself will not help with getting the prospect to read your message. But if you begin your email with something more formal like "Dear [first name]" or "Dear Ms. [last name]", the prospect will be more likely to view the message as junk.

EMAIL STRATEGIES

There are some fairly basic and easy to implement steps that you can take to greatly improve your efficiency and effectiveness when it comes to how you use email as a sales tool.

Email Templates

When prospecting, you are going to find yourself in the same situations over and over again as you are likely to face the same questions, requests, and objections. Applying that to email, you will need the same types of emails again and again – you will need to email the prospect before you call, after you briefly talk to them, after you leave a voicemail, etc.

These emails will usually look fairly similar and as a result, you should not be writing these out from scratch every time you need to send one. A more efficient approach is to create and utilize email templates for the different situations that you might face. These are essentially emails that have been prepopulated and you can quickly just add the prospect's name and make any minor modifications that are needed.

You can either keep your templates in a folder on your computer or in your email system and just pull them up and dump in an email when you need to send one of the common messages. Although, the most efficient process would be to have your templates stored and ready for use directly in your CRM (customer relationship management system) where you can quickly send them out with a couple clicks of a mouse.

We recommend that you build at least three email templates:

1. Pre-Call Emails

If you are trying to improve your ability to connect with the prospect, you can always try to send an email before your make your cold call. This is a brief email that introduces yourself and possibly highlights the value that you offer or the pain that you resolve. If you see yourself emailing prospects before you call them, you should definitely have a template specifically designed for this scenario.

The primary goal of this email would be to invoke some sort of a response and a secondary goal will be to educate the prospect a little on whom you are and why you are reaching out to them so that when you call, you are not starting from the very beginning.

2. Post-Call Emails

As we discussed in Chapter 6 on objections, one of the most common objections that you will face is for prospects to ask you to send them some information. And while we need to try to get around this objection, sometimes you just need to send the prospect an email with some information.

How much information you send and what type of information you send is something that you will need to think about. Your prospect will probably want you to send an email that clearly lists out what you sell so that they can quickly determine that they do not need what you offer. If you agree with the email fundamentals previously outlined, you should not give the prospect too much information and instead focus on the value you offer and pain you resolve.

Having a post-call email template that is ready to go can help to save a tremendous amount of time. And even if the prospect does not ask you to send him an email with more info, following up a call with a post-call email can always be a good habit to get into.

3. Post-Voicemail Emails

We will talk more about voicemail in Chapter 19, but one thing that can help you to improve your connect rate is to follow up your voicemails with an email. With that being the case, having a template that you can fire away right when you finish leaving a voicemail can not only help to improve your efficiency, it can also help you to improve your odds of connecting with the prospect. From a content standpoint, the post-voicemail can be fairly similar to your post-call email in terms of content.

Email Threads

An extremely effective email tactic is to create email threads. Email threads are multiple emails that are somewhat tied together and go out to the prospect spread across a period of time. For example, you can create a post-call email thread that includes an email to be sent right after the call, then second email that will go out to the prospect a week later, and then a third email that will go out two weeks later.

The threads are more than just repetitive emails as each individual email will typically be slightly different including new and additional information. For example, you might focus the first email on the pain that you resolve and that is it. This will allow you to brief and create a little curiosity. You can then build off of that on the second email to touch on the value that you have to offer. And then in a third email, you can begin to get to some of your core building interest points. Stitching those emails together and sending them to a prospect spread across a few weeks' time is what we call an email thread.

There are a couple of key benefits to doing this. First, by using multiple messages, you are able to share more information with the prospect as you are able to spread it out across multiple messages. Not only does this improve the odds of the prospect reading more information – he would never read all of the information if it were in one message, but it also helps him to retain and absorb the information since he is exposed to it at different times versus all at once. Another benefit from using email threads is the prospect will continue to receive emails from you, and in an environment where prospects don't answer their phone and read emails, these repetitive attempts can drastically improve your ability to get his attention and improve your connect rate.

You can turn any of the three email templates mentioned into email threads that include multiple emails. For example, you can send a pre-call email and then follow that by trying to call the prospect. But if you are not able to get a hold of the prospect, you can then send additional emails in the thread out to the prospect until you are able to get through. And the same flow can be applied to sending a post-call email after a brief conversation or after leaving a voicemail message. In all of these scenarios, you can improve your connect rate by sending an email thread that will include multiple emails being sent out to the prospect at different times. Automating the delivery of the emails and email threads is very helpful and we will discuss that later in this chapter.

Marketing Emails

Up until this point, we have primarily been discussing sales emails. When we say sales emails, we refer to emails that are sent during prospecting and typically have a personal design and work best when they give off a one-to-one impression. There is also a place in your email strategy for marketing emails and these are less personal and perfectly OK appearing as one-to-many.

An example of a marketing email is one that a sales person or a company sends out to a mass list and the overall message is one that is applies to a general audience. These emails often have some cosmetics wrapped around them to improve their appeal and usually have a design that includes borders, columns, and images.

Content Marketing

One main principle that can be effective with marketing emails is to use an approach where you are giving value as opposed to taking value. An example of giving value is providing the prospect with helpful information, like an article with helpful tips that your ideal prospect will find useful and be interested in. An example of taking value is when you try to promote and sell your products.

If you produce content in the form of an article or blog post, you can send that information in the form of a marketing email out to a mass list of prospects. Build these emails so that a portion of the content is in the email and the full content piece is located on your corporate website. This will help you to lead interested prospects to your website and increase your website traffic and leads. You can also follow up your marketing emails with a cold call and this multi-touch approach can help to improve your connect rate.

One way to ensure that you are building content that your prospects will be interested in is to identify a list of common pain points that your prospects are likely to have. Once you have that list, you can create a content piece around each pain point and use the list as an editorial calendar for your content marketing strategy.

Email Blasts

One thing that can really accelerate your results is when you are able to send out your emails to a large list of prospects through an all at once email blast. For your sales email templates, this really only applies to your pre-call templates as your post-call and post-voicemail will all be one email at a time. Being able to incorporate email blasts will drastically improve your efficiency and your connect rate.

EMAIL LOGISTICS

We have just outlined a lot of different things to do and consider when it comes to using email as an effective sales tool. There are a few logistical details that need to be outlined in order to make all of that work.

Sending Emails

There are different types of systems that you can use to send and manage your emails. Of course you can use whatever email system or interface you currently use to send and receive email. Although, when it comes to sending email threads and email blasts, you may be better served using a system that has more email marketing and email automation functionality.

Email Marketing Software

One option that you have for automating your email is using a commercial email marketing software solution. There are a large number to choose from and just about all of them will let you easily upload your list of target prospects, build out your emails, and then manage the delivery of your messages.

Standard functionality in all of these systems is going to be the ability to track "opens" and "clicks". Opens are the prospects that opened your email and clicks are when a prospect clicks on a link inside your email.

This is valuable data as it tells you which prospects are most interested. For example, if you send an email that has a content piece on a particular pain point and a prospect clicks the link in the email that takes him to read more on the subject, that click tells you that the prospect has at least some level of interest in resolving that pain point. This means that you should cold call this prospect ahead of prospects that did not click on anything in the email. In a way, tracking the clicks helps your prospects to become self-qualified.

CRM Software

Most CRM systems will have functionality that will allow you to create email templates. This will save you a tremendous amount of time as you can typically just click on your contact, select a template, and quickly send a message out. Where some CRM systems fall short is in the area of email marketing and are sometimes not be able to automate future emails and send out mass blasts. SalesNexus is an example of a CRM solution that has strong email marketing and email automation capabilities built in.

There are some fairly significant benefits to using a CRM for your email activities. First, the CRM is where all of your target contacts are loaded up and stored so that is where all of your phone numbers and email addresses are located and this makes it a little easier and quicker to fire off emails, whether sending one at a time or performing a mass blast. In addition, all of the valuable data that is produced (the opens and clicks) will be stored in your CRM with all of your contacts and documented as notes and history. Having all of this information in one place will not only simplify and save time, it will also enable you to make better decisions and prioritize your calls, all leading to a better connect rate.

Email Addresses

You may be thinking at this point that this all sounds great but what if you do not have the prospect's email address. The first thing that you can do to try to help with this is to use a lead source that provides contacts with email addresses. LeadFerret is an example of a business contact directory service that includes an email address with each contact. This can help you to build a large list of target prospects with email addresses and can help if you plan to send a pre-call email thread or mass marketing emails.

Another option that you have is to actually guess the prospect's email, which is actually easier than it sounds. The main thing that helps with this is that many companies use similar naming convention styles for their email formats and below are some of the more common types:

- [first name].[last name]@[company website address]
- [first name]_[last name]@[company website address]
- [first initial][last name]@[company website address]
- [first name]@[company website address]
- [last name]@[company website address]

If you have the contact's first and last name and know her company's website address, you can take one of these common email formats and send an email with a guessed email address. If you guess wrong, the email will come back to you as undeliverable. When that happens, you know that your guess was wrong and you can resend the email with a different guess. You can continue to repeat this process until the email does not bounce back and that is when you know that you got it right.

Another way to try to figure out the format for the company's email addresses is to go to Google and put *@[company website address] in the search field and perform a search. The results will be pages that have random email addresses on them and you can scan the pages to try to find an example of an email address to try to identify the company's standard email format. You can then copy the format and just replace with your target prospect's name and this will decrease the number of guesses that you have to make.

19

VOICEMAIL

SOLVING THE MESSAGE MYSTERY

*Tact is the art of making a point
without making an enemy.*

Isaac Newton

It was pointed out in Chapter 8 that you could sometimes spend 50 percent of your cold calling time dealing with gatekeepers. Building off of that assumption and expectation, it is also safe to expect to spend about 30 percent of your cold calling time getting directed to prospects' voicemail boxes. This high percentage is based on the fact that not only are prospects easily able to see who is calling through caller ID and let calls rollover to voicemail, but also because prospects are often too busy to answer their phone. With all of this being the case, it can be helpful to have some sort of plan and logic for how to handle voicemail systems.

UNDERSTAND THE PROSPECT

Before we discuss what to do with voicemail, let's stop and try to understand the prospect and the environment in which your message will be listened to. This is very important, as an ability to understand the prospect can clearly impact your actions and how you decide to communicate.

For example, let's consider that you have a prospect who has a very light workload and a job that is somewhat boring and slow-paced. This could mean that the prospect's phone never rings and he rarely has voice-mails waiting for him. The picture that we can build of this situation is an environment that is fairly quiet and a prospect who could be labeled as very available. If this is the type of person you are calling, you could leave a very long message that is not very tight in terms of messaging, and not only could you expect the prospect to listen and pay attention to your message, he might even be likely to call you back.

But in reality, the prospects you are calling are probably the exact opposite of this, which means they could be in an environment that is very busy and fast-paced, where the phone rings a lot and where there are numerous messages being left every day. This is a safe assumption to make because, if you are calling qualified prospects, they may have some amount of decision-making power. If they have decision-making power, not only does this mean that they will likely have a busy schedule dealing with decisions and managing their operations, but they are likely the people whom other sales people are calling to sell products to as well. If you understand that this is the landscape into which you are calling, you can begin to build and utilize an approach that makes the most sense.

ASSUME "NO CALL BACK"

As you begin to understand how hectic a target prospect's environment and voicemail queue might be, you can begin to see that there's a good chance they might not call you back. This may sound pessimistic, but the reality is that the prospect not calling back is an outcome that has a very high probability, and there are three logical reasons why.

1. The prospect has no interest

The first and most obvious reason that the prospect is likely to not call you back is that he has no interest in talking to you or buying what you are selling. It may sound negative to have this thought floating around in your mind, but the fact is that you simply might not have had the opportunity to create real interest. Email and voicemail are not effective tools for building interest, and if those are the only ways that you have been able to communicate with the prospect up until this point, the prospect might have a low to nonexistent level of interest. As a result, there might be a low to nonexistent probability of him returning any voicemail messages that you leave.

2. The prospect is interested but is too busy

Moving on to a more optimistic mindset, if you assume that your messages or previous conversations have triggered genuine interest and the prospect internally acknowledges the need to call you back, he still might not take action due to the size of his workload. If you put yourself into the mind of your prospects, you can see that if a prospect actually writes down a note to call you back with your phone number, it is still very realistic that he could simply be too busy to ever get to the task of calling you back.

This lack of action or lack of response says nothing about the qualification of the prospect or the level of interest that he has. As we have noted, the prospects we sell to are simply busier now than they ever have been, and they typically work in very fast-paced environments with plenty of noise and distractions.

3. The prospect is interested but taking a passive role

Another reason that a prospect might not call back is that he might have a decent level of interest and want to talk with you, but he is taking a more passive role and will just wait for you to call him back. Most prospects have dealt with many different sales people and they know that not only is it part of the sales person's job to call the prospect, but most sales people will be persistent and continue to make multiple attempts to try to reach a prospect. That being the case, a prospect could realistically take no action after hearing a voicemail based solely on the intention of just waiting for the sales person to call back.

VOICEMAIL TACTICS

At this point we have discussed two assumptions: 1) a large percentage of the calls we make can end up in voicemail systems, and 2) the most common outcome from a voicemail message is no response. If we feel those are anywhere close to reality and take them into consideration, here are some tactics that could make sense for how to handle voicemail.

Adjust Expectations

The first thing that you can do on the subject of voicemails is to adjust your expectations. If it is very likely that messages are not going to get returned, you can understand your prospect better and therefore understand why they are not calling you back. This can not only help you to avoid getting upset and frustrated, but can also help you to avoid misreading levels of interest and quality of leads when there is no call back.

Modify the Goal

If there was a decent chance that someone was going to return your voicemail, then a good goal of a message would be to trigger a call back. But if it is safe to assume that the prospects might be more likely to not respond regardless of what is said in the message and their level of interest, then you could shift from trying to get a call back to a strategy that is designed to educate the prospect. For example, if you have never spoken with the prospect and it is truly a cold call in terms of the fact that she does not know who you are, you can use the message to introduce yourself, share some sort of value statement to let the prospect know the value that you have to offer and why it might make sense for her to talk with you at some point. The prospect might not call back, but after she hears this type of message she might know a little more about you when she receives future emails or phone calls from you.

You can use this same logic when receiving voicemail boxes beyond the cold call stage of the sales cycle as you can use the message to educate the prospect on why you are calling and where you are in the sales process. For example, you can leave a message that summarizes why you are calling back, what occurred during your last discussion, what the options and directions discussed were, and what was last agreed to. Again, the prospect might not call back but you are at least educating, or more accurately reminding, the prospect on what you are doing and the direction that was agreed to.

Message or no Message

A very common question that can be asked or decision point to arrive at is whether or not to leave a voicemail when cold calling. The best response to that conundrum is that it depends, and the best action may differ from situation to situation. But there are a couple of questions that you can look at to try to help you determine what to do.

How important or urgent is the need to talk with the prospect?

This is going to be another one of those counterintuitive relationships: the more important or urgent the need is to talk with the prospect, the less it might make sense to leave a voicemail message. This is because if you leave a message, whether you say it or not, there is a transfer of the responsibility to make the next call over to the prospect. In other words, in most scenarios, after you leave a voicemail, you are supposed to wait for the prospect to return your call. If you call back, you are skipping the prospect's turn to act and if you don't want to send any negative vibes, you will need a certain amount of time to pass before calling again.

If you do not leave a voicemail, you have more freedom to frequently call the prospect until he answers. As a result, if it is important or urgent that you talk with a prospect, it is sometimes better to not leave a voicemail.

How many other prospects do we have to call?

Another question to look at is how many total prospects are on your list to call. Is the list extremely long or fairly short? This may also sound counterintuitive because if the list is long, it may make more sense to leave a message.

You would think that a short list means that each prospect is more important and as a result, each should get more attention, and this should include leaving voicemail messages. But another way to look at it is that a short list of prospects means that you will be able to focus on calling back frequently until you reach the prospect. When you are either extremely busy or are working on a long list and don't know when you are going to be getting back to calling that particular prospect, it may make sense to leave a brief message, since you know that there is a chance that you are not going to be calling him again in the near future.

Keep the Message Short

Since your prospects are busy and could likely have a number of messages to listen to when they come across yours, keep your message as brief as possible. Try to keep the total message between twenty and thirty seconds. The longer it drags on, the more likely the prospect is to hit delete before reaching the end. And if your contact information is at the end of the message and the message has a length that decreases the chances of the prospect listening to its entirety, this could have a very negative impact on the probability of the prospect returning the call.

Clearly Share Contact

Even if you have zero expectation of a call back, you still need to share your contact information in the message, and there are some key things that you can do to make it easier for the prospect to get your information. The absolute worst scenario would be for a prospect to have interest in returning a call, but then have difficulty extracting the contact information from the message.

At a minimum, you will want to share your name, the company you represent, and your best call back number. It is important to picture somebody writing down your contact info as you are sharing it on the message to help you from speaking too fast. Another tactic is to repeat your contact to ensure that your prospect can get your info without having to rewind the message by saying something like below:

> "...and you can reach me at 555-555-5555. Again, this is Susan Tyler with Anchor Wells, 555-555-5555."

Some experts have advised to leaving your call back number at the beginning of the message right after you say your name so that if the prospect wants to hear the number again, he can just rewind back to the beginning. That is sound logic but it is a little awkward receiving a message where the caller says their phone number in the beginning of their message.

Follow with an Email

After leaving a message, a best practice is to always follow that step with an email to the prospect. This can be a powerful tactic because you are basically hitting the prospect twice with two different communication methods. Doing so can increase your chances of getting noticed and getting your message heard.

Email is also a much easier format for the prospect to use to extract your contact information, as it is usually listed at the bottom of the email in a signature. In addition, an email is something that is much easier for the prospect to file away and save for a later date compared to a note jotted down on a pad of paper that might get thrown away or lost.

It can also be good to let the prospect know at the end of the voicemail message that you will also be sending him an email with your information. When he hears this, he can then know that he does not need to write down all of your details, since there will be an email on the way. And he might appreciate that your thoroughness is saving him energy and time. This minor step might not only help with getting through to the prospect, but it could also be a first minor step to building rapport.

Putting the Car in Reverse

If you reach a voicemail box for a prospect and decide the best decision is to not leave a message, you can sometimes press "0" during the prospect's voicemail message and get routed back to the gatekeeper, depending on the phone system. If you are able to this, you can let the gatekeeper know that you received the target prospect's voicemail greeting and use that as an opportunity to try to get additional information. Valuable information to try to gather may be to find out the best time or way to connect with the target prospect, or you may try to find out what other contacts in the organization you could or should try to speak with since the target prospect is not available.

20

CLOSE

SECURING COMMITMENT

You miss 100 percent of the shots that you don't take.
WAYNE GRETZKY

One of the most important steps in a sales process is the closing of the sale. Applying that to cold calling, the close that you are initially going for is reaching agreement to keep talking and to transition to an official first conversation. The good news is that there are many tactics that you can implement to directly and indirectly improve your ability to consistently close.

DIRECT CLOSING TECHNIQUES

There are some very direct closing techniques that you can use in which you deliver either questions or statements to try to get the prospect to move forward.

Assumptive Close

An assumptive close is to use language that assumes the prospect wants to move forward. An example of this while cold calling would be to say, "What time would you like me to schedule your free consultation?" This is assumptive if the prospect has not yet expressed interest in moving forward.

> **Pros:** This can help to push a prospect along before he can object or change his mind. This may also motivate action from a prospect who might be in a neutral or on-the-fence.

> **Cons:** This level of aggressiveness might sub-communicate negative vibes to the prospect, and this could negatively impact rapport and credibility. This approach could push away a prospect who was in a neutral position.

Alternative Close

An alternative close is a tactic in which you provide the prospect with two options for a next step and then ask which he prefers. For example, "We have workshops available on Monday afternoon and Thursday morning. Which one would you prefer to be signed up for?"

> **Pros:** This can help to push a prospect along before he can object or change his mind. This may also motivate action from a prospect who might be in a neutral or on-the-fence.

> **Cons:** This level of aggressiveness might sub-communicate negative vibes to the prospect, and this could negatively impact rapport and credibility. This approach could push away a prospect who was in a neutral position.

Trial Close

Trial closing is a test close that checks in with the prospect to get his thoughts, opinions, and feelings. This tactic is designed to get feedback and information more than to get the prospect's final decision, but a final decision could result from a trial close. Below are some examples of questions that are trial closes:

"What do you think of what we have discussed so far?"

"How would that feature help your operation?"

"Is this something you could see your employees using?"

"Do you want to continue forward with these discussions?"

"What direction do you want to go in from here?"

"Are we heading in the right direction?"

By gathering information through these questions and learning what is going on in the prospect's head, you can identify if the prospect is comprehending and agreeing with what is being discussed. This is very valuable information to have, as not only is it good to know that you are heading in the right direction, but if you happen to identify that there are challenges, objections, or concerns for the prospect, you can make real-time adjustments to address those instead of just continuing to try to power forward.

Trial closing is not just something that you should do at the end of the sales cycle or at the end of the cold call because you can benefit from checking in with the prospect every step of the way.

Pros: Trial closing improves qualifying and deal management by collecting valuable information. This tactic can also improve rapport, as it can sub-communicate positive vibes like confidence, experience, abundance, and putting the prospect's interests first.

Cons: One challenge with this tactic is that it gives the prospect an opportunity to share negative thoughts and gives him more control. If you have not been successful in building interest and rapport and you then invite the prospect to share thoughts, you might not get the answers that you want to hear.

Letting the Prospect Lead

Similar to trial closing, another closing technique to use is to let the prospect lead by asking what direction he wants to go in. This closing tactic is accomplished by simply asking questions like:

"What would you like to do next?"

"What direction would you like to go in?"

"Do you want to continue talking about this?"

"When would you like to talk again?"

This is a very powerful closing tactic, but it is critical to execute well in other areas already discussed in this book like qualifying, identifying pain, building interest, and building rapport when using this technique. If you have not covered some of the other bases, you may not be able to completely leave it up to the prospect to determine what to do next as his first thought might be to not move forward.

Pros: Letting the prospect lead is a very unthreatening way to interact with prospects and this can help to build rapport. This can also increase the quality of leads as you will know that all of the prospects you are meeting with want to be there and were not pressured to do anything.

Cons: One challenge with this tactic is that it gives the prospect more control. If you have not been successful in building interest and rapport and then you give control to the prospect to chose what direction to go in, he might not chose to go in the right direction.

Turn Questions into Statements

In Chapter 16, we discussed adding question marks to the end of statements to add more curiosity to our tonality. As a closing tactic, we can do the exact opposite by changing questions into statements. This can help to motivate movement and commitment. For example:

Question: *"Would you like to meet next week?"*

Statement: *"We should meet next week."*

This tactic may appear to conflict with the previous move of asking the prospect what direction to go in, but the two tactics can actually be used together by being delivered at different times. For example, you could deliver statements to motivate action and then confirm the direction before moving forward by asking the prospect what he would like to do next. Below is a demonstration of this.

Statement: *"We should meet next week."*

Discussion: (Discussion around meeting options) *"Those are some different directions we can go."*

Letting Prospect Lead: *"What direction would you like to go?"*

Pros: This tactic displays confidence and can motivate action.

Cons: One downside to this tactic is that you are telling the prospect what to do instead of letting the prospect tell you what to do. This can motivate action but you may create action with prospects who are not fully on board and this could decrease the quality of leads.

INDIRECT CLOSING TECHNIQUES

It is not uncommon for there to be a lot of attention, pressure, and stress on closing and being a better closer. While closing is actually the most important event during the sales cycle, it can be made easier and sometimes take care of itself if you execute well in areas outside of closing:

Communicating Value: If you effectively communicate value, you will get the prospect's attention and build interest. The better you are able to execute with this, the more interested the prospect will be, and this will make closing easier.

Qualifying the Prospect: The better you qualify the prospect, the better you will be at screening prospects who fit from the ones who don't. The result is that you will be working with prospects who are a good fit with what you have to offer, which will improve your close rate.

Disqualifying Neutral Prospects: Similarly, if you use the disqualifying tactic to push away prospects who are on the fence, you will instigate movement on qualified prospects and screen out prospects who do not have potential to move forward. These two events will have a positive impact on your close rate.

Uncovering Pain: The better you execute with uncovering and magnifying pain, the more motivated the prospect will be to make a change. The more he believes that what you have offer that can decrease this pain, the more motivated the prospect will be to move forward, and this can improve your close rate.

Building Rapport: If you effectively build rapport with prospects, not only will you stand to improve your ability to close because prospects buy from people they like, but you will also be able to improve your control over the sales cycle because prospects will be more likely to be responsive when you need to communicate and meet with them.

Building Interest: You will need to create interest on the prospect's side to have any chance of getting commitment to move forward. The better you are able to consistently build interest and communicate how you can help, how you differ from the competition, and why doing nothing is not an option, the higher your close rate will be.

Credibility: The more effective you are at establishing credibility, the more comfortable the prospect will be with moving forward and making a commitment. This too can have a positive impact on your close rate.

21

REFLECTION

REFLECTING
BACK TO MOVE FORWARD

When you lose, don't lose the lesson.
DALAI LAMA

One of the many reasons that cold calling can be challenging is that each person you call and each conversation you have is unique and unpredictable. There are some things you can do to better prepare for the calls that you make, but at the end of the day you never know how the call is going to go. With that being the case, one way to continue to grow and improve results is to embrace a concept of reflection after each call you make.

After a cold call ends, it can be very productive to stop for a minute to reflect on how the call went in an attempt to identify what could have gone better. While there are many different scenarios that you can come across, the same kinds of interactions tend to recur again and again. Therefore, if you can consciously reflect on what happened on the previous call and identify what you could have done better, you can improve your performance when similar scenarios occur on future calls.

REFLECTING ON ENCOUNTERED OBJECTIONS

As discussed in Chapter 6, you are likely to face objections on every cold call. And whether the objection brought the call to an end or not, it can be helpful to reflect on the objections that a prospect used so that you can continue to improve your technique moving forward. There are three steps that you can go through when reflecting on objections:

1. Identify objections received

Reflect back to identify what objections the prospect had during your call. What did the prospect say to try to take control of the conversation? Did she deliver an objection that brought the call to an end?

Once you identify the objections, reconcile those with your list of anticipated objections. If there are any that cannot be found on our anticipated list, this is a good time to get them added so that you can begin to be more prepared on future calls.

2. Reflect on the response

Reflect on how you responded to the objections. How did the prospect respond to your responses? Are there better responses that you could have used to keep the call going?

If the objections were on the anticipated list, it can be good to look at whether or not you delivered a response that was part of your plan, and if you responded in the way that you were supposed to. You can also reflect on how the prospect reacted to your objection response to measure how well your response worked to keep the call going.

3. Strategize moving forward

Once you have evaluated both the objections you faced and the responses you used, you can strategize how best to handle objections on future calls. If you already had responses scripted, this step may involve adjusting or tweaking our plan based on your assessment of how the prospect reacted to your responses. If there are new objections encountered, this step could involve building responses for the new objections moving forward.

REFLECTING ON THE QUESTIONS YOU ASKED

In addition to reflecting on encountered objections, you can also reflect on your ability to ask the prospect good questions during the call. In a common scenario, you may have had your initial questions prepared in some sort of script or plan, but it is the second and third level of questions where it is tough to prepare and where you will likely need to improvise.

Since it is sometimes too difficult to prepare for all of the different directions in which a call can go and script out all of the different questions that can be asked, learning while making calls is one of the best ways to build a deep catalog of questions to ask. By reflecting back on previous calls, you can identify what questions could have been asked in the scenario that you just encountered. By going through this process, you can improve your ability to deliver the right questions at the right time when talking with prospects.

DOCUMENTING INFORMATION

Reflection after a cold call can also provide an opportunity to review any information that was discussed in order to finalize and document any notes. You may have made some brief short-hand notes while on the call, and the active step of reflecting after the call will help to get you in the habit of fully listing more of the details of the conversation.

Right after a call is the best time to perform this task, as that is when the information discussed is most fresh in your head. Combined with this step could be the entering of the data into whichever customer relationship management system you use.

22

SUM

ADDING UP THE EQUATION

Perseverance is not a long race;
it is many short races one after another.

W.ELLIOTT

Up until this point in this book, we have outlined and provided details on all of the variables of the Cold Calling Equation. Now it is time for the SUM section of the book which actually has a dual-meaning: not only does this serve as the summation all of the variables in the equation, but this chapter also serves as a summary of everything that we have discussed up to this point.

Goal (+)

By improving your focus on the best goal during a cold call, which should be to get the prospect to transition from a cold call to a conversation more than trying to fully sell the prospect on your products and services, you can increase the probability of moving forward beyond the cold call. This has an addition (+) effect on your results, as it can increase the quantity of first conversations that you have.

Value (x)

By transitioning from talking about products and company details to more effectively communicating the value that you offer and deliver, you stand to improve your ability to get prospects' attention and build interest. This variable has a multiplication (x) effect, as it can make every cold call that you make better and more powerful.

Target (÷)

If you are able to clearly identify the ideal prospect and where it makes the most sense to spend your energy and time, you can then build a more focused target for your efforts. This has a division (/) effect on what you are currently doing, as you will essentially be dividing the total market that you have to go after and then just focusing on the segments where your time fits best.

Qualify (-)

Time is limited so you must focus as much time on prospects who have a good chance of moving forward and decrease your time spent with those who don't. Effectively qualifying will help with this. Qualifying has a subtraction (-) effect on the prospects you currently deal with, as you will be subtracting prospects whom you might have normally dealt with, but who do not have a likelihood of ever moving forward with a purchase.

Objections (+)

You will face objections on just about every cold call. Being able to effectively deal with these will have an addition (+) effect, as it will increase the quantity of cold calls that you are able to establish and keep going.

Disqualify (x)

Disqualifying prospects has a multiplication (x) effect, as it not only provokes idle prospects to move forward, it also decreases time that could be wasted and helps to build rapport and trust.

Gatekeeper (+)

You can sometimes spend over half of your time cold calling dealing with gatekeepers. If you are able to effectively turn them from enemies to allies, we can see an addition (+) effect, as there will likely be an increase in your total number of high-quality cold calls.

Pain (x)

In order to increase your time spent with qualified prospects that have a real chance of making a change and a purchase, you must be effective at uncovering pain that they are having. By spending time with qualified prospects and getting productive conversations going primarily around the areas that where there are challenges or have room for improvement, you should see a direct improvement in your leads produced, pipeline management, and close rate and these combined effects can have a multiplication (x) effect on your results.

Interest (x)

You must build a little interest on a cold call before you try to close the prospect for moving on to the next step. Without doing this, it is like trying to reel in a fish that has not fully bitten down on the hook. By improving your ability to trigger interest, you can see a multiplication (x) effect on results, as it will have a direct impact on your leads produced and close rate.

Rapport (x)

It is critical to be able to establish rapport with prospects. Not only do people buy from people they like, but also your ability to build rapport will make the prospects more responsive and more open with information sharing throughout the sales cycle. This can have a multiplication (x) effect on results, as it can improve every conversation that you have.

Credibility (+)

Being able to establish and display credibility can help with not only getting a prospect's attention, but also securing her commitment. This can have an addition (+) effect by increasing quality calls, leads, and closed deals.

Script (x)

It is no surprise that the more prepared you are in terms of knowing what to say and ask, the better you will perform. This variable has a multiplication (x) effect, as it can make every cold call that you make better and more powerful.

Inner Game (+)

By better dealing with the mental aspects and challenges that come with sales and cold calling, you will be able to better manage and optimize your activity level and longevity. By improving activity, you will see an addition (+) effect, as it is likely that your activity levels and total number of cold calls will increase.

Activity (+)

Of course, you have to get in the game and stay in the game in order to improve results. Improving the activity level will have an addition (+) effect, as it is likely that your activity levels and total number of cold calls will increase.

Voice (x)

When communicating over the phone, your voice plays such an important role in how you are received by the other person. If you can find ways to improve your voice and tonality, you can stand to make every single conversation better. If you can make every conversation better, you can stand to see a multiplication (x) effect on your results.

Connect (x)

You can have the best product on the market and a really effective script to get meetings and generate interest, but if you are not able to get a hold of the prospects, all of that will not do you any good. Simply connecting will sometimes be more than half the battle, and if you are able to use tools, tactics, and processes that enable you to improve your ability to connect, you can see a multiplication (x) effect on our results.

Email (+)

Email can be an effective tool to use when trying to improve the connect rate. By successfully incorporating email into your cold calling strategy, you will improve your connect rate and this can have a positive and addition (+) effect on the number of meetings you are able to schedule.

Voicemail (+)

If you can expect to spend about 50 percent of your cold calling time dealing with gatekeepers, you can also expect to spend 20 to 30 percent of your time reaching prospects' voicemail boxes. Having better logic and approach for what to do with these calls can have a positive and addition (+) effect on results.

Reflection (x)

Whether a cold call goes well or not, there is so much to learn from each conversation. What did you do well? What could you have done better? What did the prospect say to get off the phone? By reflecting back, you can improve moving forward, and this can have a multiplication (x) effect on your skills and our future conversations.

Close (+)

If you add up all of the variables of the Cold Calling Equation, you stand to not only see an increase in total closes, but it is likely that closing in general will get easier. This improvement can have an addition (+) effect with an increase in total closes.

Sum (=)

When you factor in positive energy and investment in any of the variables of this equation, the results add up to improved cold calling, improved quality and quantity of leads, and improved close rate. The sum of all of that is improved performance and increased sales results.

ABOUT AUTHOR

The foundation for all of Michael Halper's teachings is twenty years working on the frontlines in sales, marketing, and customer service roles. During that time, he worked for many organizations, for many different managers, and saw just about everything in terms of what a sales person should and should not do. He experienced both failure and success, learning from every experience, from every deal, and from every interaction. It was fighting in the trenches day in and day out where he learned what it takes to be successful.

Halper combines his real-world experience with a strong educational background including a BBA in Marketing, an MBA in Management from the University of Houston, a Graduate Certificate in Executive Coaching, and is currently working on a Masters of Science in Organizational Behavior at the University of Texas at Dallas. He is also a certified professional coach currently holding an ICF Associate Certified Coach credential.

In 2009, Halper founded Launch Pad Solutions, LLC, a sales training and services firm. Launch Pad helps business owners and sales professionals to increase sales by improving the area of sales prospecting. Launch Pad helps to improve the strategy and direction through consulting, training, and coaching. And for many businesses that don't want to deal with prospecting, Launch Pad will take that off of their plate and perform the activities needed through an outsourced telesales operation.

After years of building sales prospecting campaigns, Halper developed a level of expertise in developing sales messaging and began to develop logic and tools to assist with this area. Out of this work evolved the SalesScripter solution, a web-based tool that will help a business owner or sales person to develop a major portion of their sales messaging and sales strategy. In 2012, through a partnership with SalesNexus, LLC, Halper founded SalesScripter, LLC, a business and solution with the charter of helping to make prospecting easier for sales professionals around the globe.

Halper is also President of the American Association of Inside Sales Professionals (AA-ISP) Houston Chapter. AA-ISP is a global organization that is focused on helping those that work in inside sales to be more effective and successful.

REFRERENCES

The concepts of the book are not solely the original creation of ideas and thoughts produced by the author. The foundation for the development of these ideas and principles are years of experience working in the trenches making cold calls while working for many different companies, working for many different sales managers, learning a variety of sales training programs and methodologies, completing formal academic programs, and through a large amount of self-education through trial and error, sales books, and researching the industries best gurus.

SALES TRAINING PROGRAMS

The following are sales programs that the author has attended that have had a positive impact on his career and as a result have helped him to be a successful sales coach.

Ovation Sales Training – www.ovationsalestraining.com

Conceptual Selling – Miller Heiman www.millerheiman.com

Strategic Selling – Miller Heiman www.millerheiman.com

Sandler Sales Methodology – Sandler Sales Institute www.sandler.com

Holden Sales Methodology – Holden International
www.holdenintl.com

University of Houston – Sales Excellence Institute
www.bauer.uh.edu/SEI

University of Texas at Dallas – Executive Coaching Program
www.jindal.utdallas.edu

The Profit Specialist – Aarthun Performance Group, LTD
www.aarthun.com

SALES BOOKS

The following are books that the author has acknowledged as having an impact on his success as a sales professional and influenced his current coaching and teachings.

The Solution Selling Fieldbook – Keith Eades, James Touchstone, Timothy Sullivan

S.P.I.N. Selling – Huthwaite

Getting to Yes – by Roger Fisher

Selling ASAP – Dr. Eli Jones

Selling to Big Companies – Jill Konrath

Let's Get Real or Let's Not Play – Mahan Khalsa

Red-Hot Cold Call Selling – Paul S. Goldner

The 7 Habits of Highly Effective People – Stephen R. Covey

Influence: Science and Practice – by Robert B. Cialdini

ACKNOWLEDGEMENTS

Below are a few individuals that has had a positive impact on the authors competence as a sales professional, as a sales coach, as a sales trainer, and as an individual.

Dave Smith – VP of Sales at Ceridian 2004 to 2010

Scott Morgan – Regional Sales Manager at Kronos 2004 to 2009

Jake Atwood – President Ovation Sales Group

Mike Kinney – VP of Sales at Ceridian 2006 to 2010

Jeff Halper – Founder and CEO at Exterior Worlds, Inc. 1988 to Present Justin Hedge – Founder and CEO at Electron Storm, LLC 2009 to Present

Brad Jones – Founder and President, Unity Recruitment 2007 to Present

Oscar Gutierrez – Senior Marketing Director, Transamerica Financial Advisors, Inc.

Steven Lumpkins – Founder and CEO, Beer Brain Trivia Entertainment, 2010 to Present

Jon Harmon – Director of Sales at BMC Software 2001 to Present

Craig Klein – Founder and CEO, SalesNexus, LLC, 2001 to Present

RECOMMENDED RESOURCES

LAUNCH PAD SOLUTIONS

Launch Pad is a sales training and services provider that helps businesses and sales professionals to improve their ability to generate leads by improving the areas of cold calling and outbound prospecting. This is a good resource for:

- Web-based and live sales training
- One-on-one sales coaching
- Sales consulting
- Appointment setting lead generation services
- Cold call outsourcing

If you found the information in this book to be helpful, Launch Pad has full training programs and services that utilize all of these concepts.

www.lp-sol.com | info@lp-sol.com | (888) 804-3756

SALESSCRIPTER

SalesScripter is a web-based tool that helps sales professionals and sales managers to develop all of their sales messaging. SalesScripter takes you through a series of questions that extract all of the key details about your products, company, and prospects. The information collected is then plugged into deep library of scripts, templates, and sales tools including:

- Cold call, first meeting, and voicemail scripts
- Pre-call and post-call email templates
- Objections responses
- Qualifying questions
- Value statements
- Your ideal prospect pain points
- Sales presentation
- And more...

The scripter utilizes all of the concepts of this book and will help you to apply and implement any of these principles to your particular situation.

www.salesscripter.com | info@salesscripter.com | (713) 802-2026

SALESNEXUS

SalesNexus is Customer Relationship Management (CRM) and Email Marketing in one easy to use solution built by sales people for sales people. SalesNexus enables sales teams to:

- Reach a wider audience through email marketing
- Pre-qualify sales leads based on email opens and clicks
- Measure campaign performance
- Automate and manage sales processes
- Measure and manage sales activities
- Forecast and manage the sales pipeline
- Build stronger, lasting customer relationships by sharing a 360 degree view of the customer with the entire team
- Access and update customer information on the go via smartphone, tablet and web
- Capture web site leads
- Archive and retrieve email correspondence.

SalesNexus provides comprehensive QuickStart programs, live training and help desk services to ensure your business achieves it's goals for growth!

www.salesnexus.com | info@salesnexus.com | (800) 862-0134

LEADFERRET

LeadFerret is the world's first 100% free business-to-business database with complete information, including e-mail addresses. Every record in LeadFerret is complete with company information, name, title, address, phone number and the more important –email addresses. Many records now even come with links to social media profiles.

The best thing about LeadFerret is ...it's FREE!

- View any or all of the 10 million+ at no cost
- You can also earn or buy points to download records directly to a spreadsheet
- Integrated with SalesNexus enabling contacts to be uploaded to your CRM with just a couple of clicks
- You will receive 500 free contacts every month when you use SalesNexus with LeadFerret

www.leadferret.com | info@leadferret.com | (866) 535-3960

Made in the USA
San Bernardino, CA
23 September 2015